Cambridge Elements

Elements in the Philosophy of Biology
edited by
Grant Ramsey
KU Leuven

WHAT IS LIFE? REVISITED

Daniel J. Nicholson
George Mason University

Shaftesbury Road, Cambridge CB2 8EA, United Kingdom

One Liberty Plaza, 20th Floor, New York, NY 10006, USA

477 Williamstown Road, Port Melbourne, VIC 3207, Australia

314–321, 3rd Floor, Plot 3, Splendor Forum, Jasola District Centre, New Delhi – 110025, India

103 Penang Road, #05-06/07, Visioncrest Commercial, Singapore 238467

Cambridge University Press is part of Cambridge University Press & Assessment, a department of the University of Cambridge.

We share the University's mission to contribute to society through the pursuit of education, learning and research at the highest international levels of excellence.

www.cambridge.org
Information on this title: www.cambridge.org/9781009124188

DOI: 10.1017/9781009127318

© Daniel J. Nicholson 2025

This publication is in copyright. Subject to statutory exception and to the provisions of relevant collective licensing agreements, no reproduction of any part may take place without the written permission of Cambridge University Press & Assessment.

When citing this work, please include a reference to the DOI 10.1017/9781009127318

First published 2025

A catalogue record for this publication is available from the British Library

ISBN 978-1-009-57891-2 Hardback
ISBN 978-1-009-12418-8 Paperback
ISSN 2515-1126 (online)
ISSN 2515-1118 (print)

Cambridge University Press & Assessment has no responsibility for the persistence or accuracy of URLs for external or third-party internet websites referred to in this publication and does not guarantee that any content on such websites is, or will remain, accurate or appropriate.

For EU product safety concerns, contact us at Calle de José Abascal, 56, 1°, 28003 Madrid, Spain, or email eugpsr@cambridge.org

What Is Life? Revisited

Elements in the Philosophy of Biology

DOI: 10.1017/9781009127318
First published online: October 2025

Daniel J. Nicholson
George Mason University
Author for correspondence: Daniel J. Nicholson, dan.j.nicholson@gmail.com

Abstract: Erwin Schrödinger's *What Is Life?* is one of the most celebrated scientific works of the twentieth century. However, like most classics, it is far more often cited than read. Efforts to seriously engage with Schrödinger's arguments are rare. This Element explores how well his ideas have stood the test of time. It argues that Schrödinger's emphasis on the rigidity and specificity of the hereditary material (which stemmed from his attempt to explain biological order from physical principles) influenced how molecular biologists conceptualized macromolecules, resulting in a deterministic, engineering view of the cell that is still popular today—even if it is increasingly at odds with experimental findings. Drawing on archival sources, this Element also uncovers Schrödinger's motivations in writing *What Is Life?* and suggests that his biological proposals are best understood in the context of his longstanding dispute with other physicists regarding the interpretation and extension of quantum mechanics.

Keywords: Erwin Schrödinger, molecular biology, order, determinism, stochasticity

© Daniel J. Nicholson 2025
ISBNs: 9781009578912 (HB), 9781009124188 (PB), 9781009127318 (OC)
ISSNs: 2515-1126 (online), 2515-1118 (print)

Contents

1 The Status of *What Is Life?* in Molecular Biology   1

2 Reconstructing the Argument in *What Is Life?*   13

3 A Critique of the Order-from-Order Principle   21

4 A Critique of the Order-from-Disorder Principle   32

5 Rethinking Schrödinger's Impact on Molecular Biology   46

6 Understanding Schrödinger's Motives in *What Is Life?*   64

7 Conclusions: *What Is Life?* 80 Years On   79

   References   82

1 The Status of *What Is Life?* in Molecular Biology

In February 1943, right in the depths of the Second World War, far away in neutral Ireland Erwin Schrödinger (Figure 1) delivered a series of public lectures at Trinity College, Dublin under the grandiose title 'What Is Life? (The Physical Aspect of the Living Cell)'. By this time, Schrödinger was already widely acclaimed as one of the most distinguished physicists of modern times.

Born in Vienna in 1887 into a cultured, middle-class family, Schrödinger's dream had been to study physics under the great Ludwig Boltzmann, one of the founders of statistical mechanics. However, when he entered the University of Vienna in 1906, he was distraught to learn that Boltzmann had taken his own life just a few weeks earlier.[1] Instead, he was taught theoretical physics by Boltzmann's successor, Fritz Hasenöhrl, and experimental physics by Franz Exner, both of whom would exert a lasting influence on Schrödinger.

After obtaining his doctorate and serving on the Italian front during the First World War, Schrödinger held a series of short-term appointments at Jena (as assistant to Max Wien), Stuttgart, and Breslau, before taking up a professorship in theoretical physics in Zurich in 1921. Five years later, at the relatively late age of thirty-eight, Schrödinger's groundbreaking discovery of wave mechanics made him one of the leading physicists of the day. In 1927, he accepted Max Planck's chair in Berlin upon the latter's retirement (and after Arnold Sommerfeld declined it), joining an extraordinary cohort of physicists that included Albert Einstein, Walther Nernst, and Max von Laue.

When the Nazis rose to power in 1933, Schrödinger renounced his chair—probably the most prestigious in the world of physics at the time—in protest. His resignation was an act of principle, as Schrödinger himself was not Jewish.[2] He accepted a temporary position as fellow of Magdalen

---

[1] Another young Viennese who was similarly disappointed upon hearing the news of Boltzmann's suicide was Ludwig Wittgenstein, who had intended to study with him after completing his secondary school education (von Wright 1955).

[2] His decision appears to have been influenced by Michael Polanyi, who invited eight leading scientists to his home, including Planck and Schrödinger, and urged that they all resign collectively in protest of the enactment of Hitler's laws. Although everyone was appalled, only Polanyi and Schrödinger ultimately gave up their posts. Polanyi's wife later recalled Planck saying that unfortunately "LAWS [sic] had to be observed and those were the laws of the land!!!" (quoted in Yoxen 1977: 131). She also recalled an after-dinner conversation in which Schrödinger pointed to a tablecloth and said: "This white tablecloth is beautiful but were I to throw a bottle of ink over it, what would it be like? To my mind, that is what Hitler has done to Germany" (quoted in Wigner and Hodgkin 1977: 416).

Figure 1 Portrait of Erwin Schrödinger (1887–1961)
(Credit: Bettmann/Getty Images)

College, Oxford, and soon after arriving in England, he received the news that he was to share the Nobel Prize in Physics with Paul Dirac.[3]

Schrödinger's time in Oxford (vividly recounted in Clary 2022; see also Hoch and Yoxen 1987) was altogether not a happy one, so when the

---

[3] Thomas Hunt Morgan won the Physiology Nobel Prize that year "for his discoveries concerning the role played by the chromosome in heredity" (www.nobelprize.org/prizes/medicine/1933/summary/), the same topic that Schrödinger would take up a decade later in his 'What Is Life?' lectures.

opportunity arose to return to his beloved homeland in 1936, he moved back to Austria to take up a chair in Graz.[4] Schrödinger later described this decision as "an extremely foolish thing to do" (Schrödinger 1992: 182), as less than two years after his return the *Anschluss* left him at the mercy of the Nazis, who had not forgotten his disgruntled departure from Germany in 1933. He wrote a public letter, published in a local newspaper, expressing his deep shame at not having realized sooner the true destiny of his homeland, in the hope that it would suffice to placate the authorities.[5] The tactic failed, and he was summarily dismissed from his post.

Schrödinger hastily fled to Rome—leaving most of his belongings behind, including his Nobel medal—and from there made his way eventually to Dublin, where he had accepted the invitation by the *Taoiseach* Éamon de Valera (himself a former mathematician) to direct the School of Theoretical Physics at the newly established Dublin Institute for Advanced Studies (DIAS). He would remain in Ireland for seventeen years, returning to his beloved Vienna for good in 1956 (shortly after the end of the Soviet occupation of Austria), where he spent his final years. He died in 1961 aged 73.[6]

DIAS was set up to provide for Schrödinger what the Princeton Institute for Advanced Studies provided for Einstein (as well as for other émigrés): a scientific haven where he could work in peace completely unencumbered by external events. Like Einstein, Schrödinger spent a great deal of his later years unsuccessfully trying to derive a unified field theory that would encompass gravitation and electromagnetism (see Halpern 2015), but he also found time to pursue many other projects. One of the statutory obligations of DIAS was the delivery of annual public lectures, and Schrödinger was more than happy to take on this responsibility on a number of occasions. For the 1943 edition, he decided to discuss the relationship between physics and biology, choosing the intriguing title 'What Is Life?'.

---

[4] Schrödinger was also offered a chair at Edinburgh in 1936. When he declined it, it was offered to Max Born, who had been forced out of his position at Göttingen and was only too happy to accept it. Born became a naturalized British subject one day before the outbreak of the Second World War, and he remained in Edinburgh until 1952.

[5] The journal *Nature* published a brief report on Schrödinger's letter (Anon 1938), which shocked his British ex-colleagues—not to mention his Jewish friends. Some assumed he had signed the letter under duress (Yoxen 1977: 142).

[6] For comprehensive accounts of Schrödinger's life and work, see the (very readable) biographies Moore 1989 and Gribbin 2013. For shorter overviews, see Heitler 1961 and Fischer 1984.

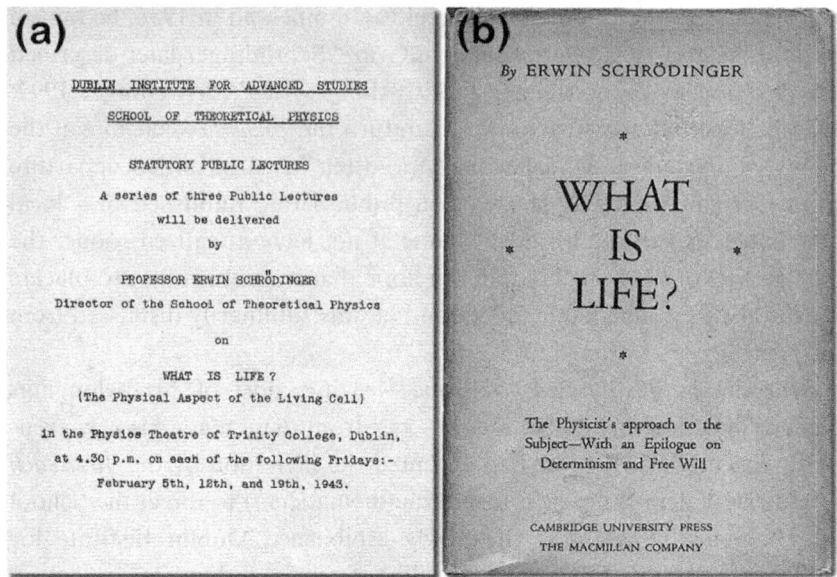

Figure 2 (a) DIAS notice for the 'What Is Life?' lectures at Trinity College, Dublin (reproduced with permission of the DIAS Archives) and (b) first American edition of *What Is Life?*

The lectures were held on three consecutive Fridays in February at the Physics Theatre of Trinity College, Dublin (Figure 2a). In attendance was de Valera, along with cabinet ministers, diplomats, socialites, and artists. The number of people who tried to crowd into the lecture hall was so great that it was necessary to repeat each lecture the following Monday for those who were turned away (Moore 1989: 395). Shortly after the lectures, Anny, Schrödinger's wife, remarked in a letter to Born that "[p]eople came one hour before the beginning [...] equiped [sic] with newspapers and books and sweets—just like for an Opera Première".[7] In total, Schrödinger estimated "an audience of about four hundred which did not substantially dwindle" between lectures (Schrödinger 1944: 1). The public excitement evoked by the lectures was reported in the *Irish Times* and even received international coverage by *Time* magazine.

As soon as he completed the lectures, Schrödinger began preparing them for publication, making arrangements with the Irish publisher Cahill & Co. He appended a brief epilogue titled 'On Determinism and Free Will', where he referred to the mystical Hindu philosophy of Vedanta in a way that

---

[7] Anne-Marie Schrödinger to Max Born, 7 March 1943, Born Papers, Berlin State Library. Intriguingly, this letter mentions that Schrödinger gave *four* lectures that were repeated, not three. What we know for sure is that the original plan was for Schrödinger to deliver three lectures, as stated in the official DIAS announcement shown in Figure 2a.

implied a rejection of Christianity. In conservative Catholic Ireland, this was perceived as offensive and unacceptable, and Schrödinger was warned that his book would not be published unless he removed the epilogue. Schrödinger refused, and the publisher decided to cancel the book's publication, despite already having produced the final proofs (Gribbin 2013: 237–238).

Undeterred, Schrödinger sent the manuscript to his friend Frederick G. Donnan, a physical chemist at University College London, who recommended Cambridge University Press as a suitable publisher and negotiated its publication with them on Schrödinger's behalf.[8] The terms of publication were settled in January 1944 and *What Is Life?* (Figure 2b) was published in December of that year.

It was an instant success. The book's captivating title, its short length, and Schrödinger's eloquent and accessible style—not to mention his world-class reputation—ensured a wide readership. Marketed at 6*s* a copy in Britain and $1.75 in the United States (where it was published by MacMillan), the book sold briskly despite wartime austerity. After the war ended, it became even more popular. Within three years, the publisher had already arranged for the book to be translated into Italian, German, Swedish, Spanish, French, and Hungarian.[9] By 1948, at least sixty-five reviews of *What Is Life?* had been published in scientific journals and the popular press (Yoxen 1979: 45).

Some of the most prominent biologists who reviewed the book included geneticists Hermann Joseph Muller, J. B. S. Haldane, and Cyril Darlington, immunologist Peter Medawar, and physicist-turned-biologist Max Delbrück. The book also prompted responses from many others. *Nature* alone published three such responses in the space of two years (Brabazon 1945; Manton 1945; Butler 1946). Among physicists, cosmologist George Gamow was deeply impressed by it. He organized a conference in 1946 sponsored by the US National Academy of Sciences in Washington, DC titled 'The Physics of Living Matter' featuring a number of outstanding physicists, including Niels Bohr, John von Neumann, Edward Teller, and Leo Szilard, as well as Delbrück, who kicked off the proceedings by stating that *What Is Life?* had been the stimulus that had brought them together (Moore 1989: 403). Later, while working on the hydrogen bomb at Los Alamos, Gamow discussed the book with his younger colleagues and two of them authored a paper stimulated by those discussions (i.e., Reitz and

---

[8] Although Donnan is seldom mentioned in scholarly discussions of *What Is Life?*, he probably did more than anybody else to shape Schrödinger's biological views, as we will see later.

[9] I thank Alejandro Fábregas-Tejeda for consulting the archival records of Cambridge University Press in Cambridge on my behalf and retrieving this information.

Longmire 1950). Gamow even used Schrödinger as the basis for one of his fictional characters in his popular science book *Mr. Tompkins Learns the Facts of Life*, describing him as:

> a celebrated Austrian physicist who once made a basic contribution to the Quantum Theory. Now he is all wound up about the fundamental problems of biology, and thinks that it's just the time for physicists to *cut in*. In fact, this *maladia biologica*, as some people call it, seems to have spread far and wide among the physicists, both theoreticians and experimentalists. And, instead of following the latest views of Dirac about the existence of light-ether, or measuring the number of delayed fission neutrons, many of them devote all of their time to breeding bacteria or cutting open the tummies of white mice. (Gamow 1953: 66)

Gamow playfully puts his finger here on what is often considered to be the book's greatest achievement, which is that it supplied an intellectual impetus for the migration into biology of many young and disaffected physicists after the war (see, e.g., Fleming 1968). By singling out the gene as the material carrier of life and showing how it could be fruitfully investigated by appealing to physical principles, *What Is Life?* is credited with helping precipitate the discoveries that resulted in the molecular revolution in biology.

Horace Freeland Judson, in his interview-based history of molecular biology, has observed that "[e]verybody read Schrödinger" (Judson 1979: 244). This is not quite the overstatement that it might seem. It is remarkable to find so many of those who are now regarded as 'founders' of molecular biology speaking—often in very personal terms—about how inspiring Schrödinger's book was. Box 1 compiles some of the most

---

BOX 1 PIONEERS OF MOLECULAR BIOLOGY ON THE INFLUENCE OF *WHAT IS LIFE?*

"During the war I took part in making the atomic bomb. When the war was ending, I, like many others, cast around for a new field of research. Partly on account of the bomb, I had lost some interest in physics. I was therefore very interested when I read Schrödinger's book *What Is Life?* and was struck by the concept of a highly complex structure which controlled living processes. Research on such matters seemed more ambitious than solid-state physics […] [and it] encouraged me to move into biology."(Wilkins 1963: 941)

"Of those who came into the subject just after the 1939–1945 war, Schrödinger's little book *What Is Life?* seems to have been peculiarly influential. […] [T]he book was extremely well written and conveyed in an exciting way the idea that, in biology, molecular explanations would not only be extremely important but also that they were just around the corner. This had been said before, but Schrödinger's book was very timely and attracted people who might otherwise not have entered biology at all." (Crick 1965: 184)

"[The book's] propagandist impact on physical scientists was very great. Their knowledge of biology was generally confined to stale botanical and zoological lore, and having one of the Founding Fathers of the new physics put the question 'What is life?' provided for them an authoritative confrontation with a fundamental problem worthy of their mettle. Since many of these physical scientists were suffering from a general professional malaise in the immediate post-war period, they were eager to direct their efforts toward a new frontier which, according to Schrödinger, was now ready for some exciting developments. In thus stirring up the passions of this audience, Schrödinger's book became a kind of *Uncle Tom's Cabin* of the revolution in biology that, when the dust had cleared, left molecular biology as its legacy." (Stent 1966: 3)

"Schrödinger [...] prophesised a new and exhilarating era for biology, particularly in the field of heredity. Just to hear one of the leaders in quantum mechanics asking 'What is life?' and then describing heredity in terms of molecular structures, inter-atomic bonds and thermodynamic stability was enough to fire the enthusiasm of certain young physicists and to bestow some sort of legitimacy on biology. Their ambition and interest were limited to a single problem: the physical basis of genetic information." (Jacob 1973: 259–260)

"I had at about that time been deeply impressed by a little book written by the great Austrian physicist Erwin Schrödinger which carried the modest title *What Is Life?* Great scientists are particularly worth listening to when they speak about something of which they know little; in their own specialty they are usually great and dull [...] The hereditary code-script? The cryptographer hidden in every soul was intrigued. 'Chromosomes!' I exclaimed. 'DNA, builder's craft! Let's work on the nose of Cleopatra!'" (Chargaff 1978: 87–88)

"I'd always had a latent interest in biology, but it was particularly Schrödinger's book that turned me on. About 1946." (Benzer, quoted in Judson 1979: 272)

"[When] I came back to the University of Chicago [in 1946, I] spotted the tiny book *What Is Life?* [...] In that little gem, Schrödinger said that the essence of life was the gene. Up until then, I was interested in birds. But then I thought, well, if the gene is the essence of life, I want to know more about it. And that was fateful because, otherwise, I would have spent my life studying birds and no one would have heard of me." (Watson 1993: 1812)

striking pronouncements to this effect. What one ought to make of such declarations is, of course, another matter, which we shall have the opportunity to examine in Section 5. Taken at face value, however, they paint a clear picture of the book's almost mythical status in molecular biology.

As Box 1 shows, all three recipients of the Nobel Prize awarded for the momentous discovery of the double helical structure of deoxyribonucleic acid (DNA)—James Watson, Francis Crick, and Maurice Wilkins—independently acknowledged Schrödinger's decisive influence. Their model of the double helix drew on the base-parity rules discovered by Erwin Chargaff, who was also inspired by the book. In 1953, shortly after the publication of the two famous *Nature* papers describing the DNA structure and its hypothesized role in the replication of genetic information (Watson and Crick 1953a, 1953b), Crick wrote a letter to Schrödinger to let him know of the importance of *What Is Life?* in their discovery (Figure 3). Watson, for his part, has repeatedly credited Schrödinger with setting him on the path to the double helix. As early as 1966, he remarked that "from the moment I read Schrödinger's *What Is Life?* I became polarized toward finding out the secret of the gene" (Watson 1966: 239). Watson has also

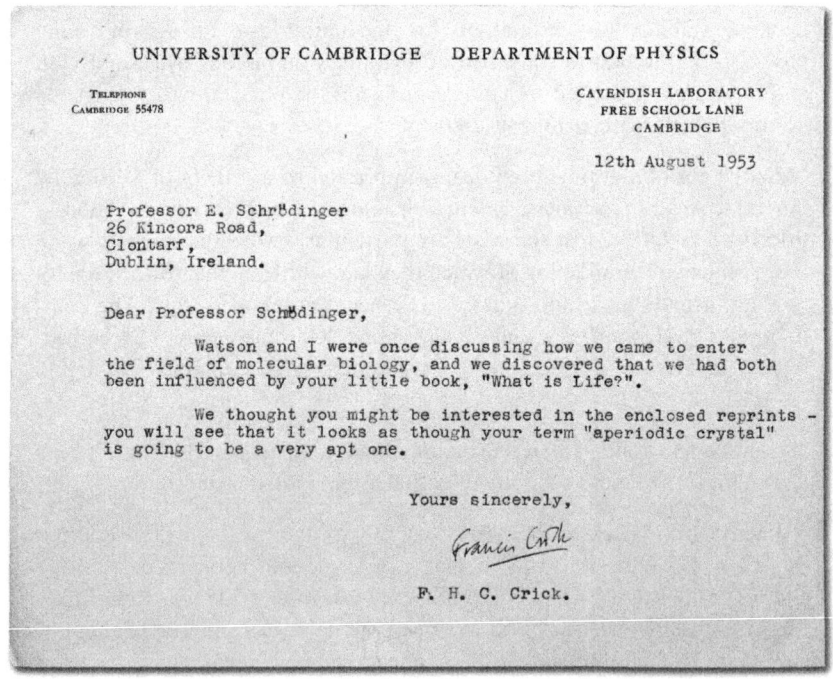

Figure 3 Letter from Francis Crick to Erwin Schrödinger, 12 August 1953 (reproduced with permission of the DIAS Archives)

mentioned that the first book he planned to write was "an elegant little successor to Schrodinger's *What Is Life?* that I would call *This Is Life*" (Watson 2001: 120), which over time developed into his landmark textbook *The Molecular Biology of the Gene* (Watson 1965).

The book also influenced Seymour Benzer and Gunther Stent, two members of Delbrück's legendary 'phage group' at Caltech, whose work was instrumental in the establishment of molecular biology.[10] Salvador Luria—another member of the phage group—recalled finding Schrödinger's book "exciting" (Stent 1968: 395). François Jacob, who shared the Nobel Prize with André Lwoff and Jacques Monod for their foundational work on gene regulation, was inspired by reading *What Is Life?* as a young man (Jacob 1988: 198) and later wrote about the book's impact on the rise of molecular biology in his well-known book on the history of biology, *The Logic of Life* (1973). Lwoff and Monod were influenced by Schrödinger as well. Lwoff's *Biological Order* (1962) includes an extended discussion of *What Is Life?* in its final chapter, and Monod's *Chance and Necessity* (1972) is even more indebted to Schrödinger's biological ideas, as we will see in Section 5. Other Nobel laureates who have recognized the book's influence include Sydney Brenner (known for his pioneering work on the genetic code and developmental genetics) and Joshua Lederberg (who discovered genetic recombination in bacteria). The latter has claimed that Schrödinger's book persuaded him early on in his career "that biology was not simply a form of 'stamp collecting' but had a real intellectual content" (quoted in Bernstein 2016: 163).[11]

The impact of *What Is Life?* has not been restricted to molecular biology. It has also inspired those exploring the biological dimensions of self-organization and non-equilibrium thermodynamics (as we will see in Section 4), as well as those interested in the biological application of information theory and cybernetics (as we will see in Section 5). In addition, it has attracted the attention of theoreticians of the calibre of Freeman Dyson (1985), Stuart Kauffman (1995), Robert Rosen (1996), Terrence Deacon (2011), and Paul Davies (2019).[12] Schrödinger's book has been discussed in

---

[10] The classic, though historiographically contentious, account of the significance of Delbrück's phage group is Cairns et al. 1966. A more recent analysis of the history of the group can be found in Summers 2023. For more general surveys of the history of molecular biology, see Olby 1974, Judson 1979, and Morange 2020.

[11] Of course, not everyone has sung the praises of *What Is Life?*. Some of the more recent appraisals of the book's place in the history of molecular biology have been decidedly more negative. We will examine these in Section 5.

[12] This list is by no means exhaustive. To mention just one more interesting example, the prominent environmental theorist James Lovelock (1986: 646) described *What Is Life?*

even wider contexts. For instance, the infamous Trofim Lysenko referred to it as a conspicuous example of 'bourgeois pseudo-science' in his political crusade against Mendelian genetics in the Soviet Union.[13]

Today, *What Is Life?* is almost always referred to as a 'classic', and it is not unusual to see it described as one of the most important and influential scientific books of the twentieth century. Given its considerable fame, it is rather ironic that the actual content of the book is seldom discussed beyond three soundbites, which are repeated *ad nauseam* in commentaries of the book. Specifically, we tend to be told that *What Is Life?* puts forward three key theses:

1. The hereditary substance is an *aperiodic crystal* that contains within it a *code-script* for development.
2. Organisms comply with the second law of thermodynamics by *feeding on negative entropy*.
3. The study of living matter is likely to eventually result in the discovery of *new laws of physics*.

Now, these statements are not wrong—Schrödinger does indeed make these three striking claims—but they do not, on their own, capture what Schrödinger is trying to accomplish in the book. In the last analysis, *What Is Life?* is not a book about genes, nor is it about entropy. Moreover, all three slogans, despite seeming straightforward enough, are frequently misunderstood, as we will see later. It is therefore a rather pressing matter to look back at the argument that Schrödinger advanced in his book, as well as to the reasons that prompted him to do so, as serious misconceptions about what the book is actually about remain to this day.

The recent celebrations commemorating the 75th anniversary of the 'What Is Life?' lectures in 1943, and of the book's publication a year later, provided a fitting occasion to revisit Schrödinger's biological ideas and to reflect on their contemporary relevance. In September 2018, Trinity

---

as "the book that most influenced my own thinking in science", going so far as to crediting it with the insight that led him to formulate his famous Gaia hypothesis: "it was by reading Schrödinger's book *What Is Life?* in the early 1960s that I first realized that planetary life was revealed by the contrast between [...] a dead planet and [...] the Earth" (Lovelock 1988: 215; see also 22–24).

[13] In a 1948 address to the Lenin Academy of Agricultural Sciences, Lysenko declared that "[t]he true ideological content of Morgan's genetics has been well revealed (to the discomfiture of our geneticists) by the physicist Erwin Schrödinger. In his book [...] he draws some philosophical conclusions from Weismann's chromosome theory, of which he speaks very approvingly" (quoted in Yoxen 1977: 168). The Soviet biochemist Alexander Oparin (1961) also examined *What Is Life?* from the perspective of dialectical materialism, offering—as one might expect—a more sober and thoughtful analysis.

College, Dublin hosted a most impressive international conference titled 'Schrödinger at 75—The Future of Biology' with a stellar roster of eminent scientists, including half a dozen Nobel laureates, and with the distinguished philosopher Daniel Dennett giving the keynote address.[14] Ostensibly an exploration of the book's legacy, the event was in fact an examination of cutting-edge research in a variety of scientific disciplines. The speakers, while dutifully acknowledging the greatness of *What Is Life?* in their introductory remarks, for the most part avoided engaging with the book in any meaningful way. It is hard not to view this as a missed opportunity.

The same is unfortunately true for most of the articles that were published to mark the occasion. Both *Nature* (i.e., Ball 2018) and *Science* (i.e., Sigmund 2019) featured special commemorative essays, which, while providing serviceable overviews of the book, its author, and its influence, did not try to offer new insights.[15] The situation is not much better when we look back at the 50th anniversary celebrations. Trinity College, Dublin also organized a commemorative conference on that occasion, which brought together a cadre of scientific celebrities, including Roger Penrose, John Maynard Smith, Stephen Jay Gould, Lewis Wolpert, Leslie Orgel, and the aforementioned Kauffman. The proceedings were published by Cambridge University Press with the title *What Is Life? The Next Fifty Years* (Murphy and O'Neill 1995). Sadly, when one inspects the individual contributions, one is disappointed to discover that, aside from Kauffman's, none really examine the contents of the book in any depth.

What we find, then, is that despite being "widely regarded as a philosophical cornerstone of modern molecular biology" (Newman 1988: 360), efforts to carefully engage with the book's argument are surprisingly rare. Most discussions of *What Is Life?* fall under two categories. Those in the first group typically summarize the book by invoking the three soundbites mentioned earlier and then rehearse the usual familiar tropes about the book's influence (e.g., Symonds 1986; Witkowski 1986; Sarkar 1991; Dronamraju 1999; Sarkar 2013; Moberg 2020). Those in the second group mischievously try to avoid examining *What Is Life?*

---

[14] All conference talks were recorded and are available to watch on YouTube. The promotional video seems more like a trailer for a Hollywood blockbuster than for an academic conference; see: https://youtu.be/TBtLQRDcvMU?si=xIFPSh29_uOrBzIe.

[15] I should note, though, that Phillip Ball's new book *How Life Works* (2023) does include a very refreshing and perceptive discussion of the relevance of Schrödinger's claims for debates about agency in one of its chapters. Rob Phillips' recent paper on *What Is Life?* also breaks away from the norm in making a serious effort to connect the book's ideas with current research in biophysics (i.e., Phillips 2021).

altogether by addressing the question 'What Is Life?' instead, which they construe capaciously enough to allow them to discuss any topic they wish (e.g., Elitzur 1995; Margulis and Sagan 1995; Fuller 2021). There are some notable exceptions, of course. Three particularly insightful commentators are Kauffman (1995, 2000), Lenny Moss (2003), and Jean-Jacques Kupiec (2009, 2010).

The comprehensive analysis of *What Is Life?* that I present in this Element builds on the insights afforded by these three authors. It also draws on a range of archival materials, and on recent (e.g., Sloan and Fogel 2011; Sloan 2012; Loison 2015) as well as old and unpublished (e.g., Yoxen 1977) historiographical studies. Having introduced Schrödinger, explained the context of his Dublin lectures, described the production of the book, and reviewed its influence on leading molecular biologists, let me now outline the four goals that I have set myself for the rest of this Element.

The first is to set the record straight on what Schrödinger is actually arguing for in *What Is Life?* (Section 2). The second is to retrospectively evaluate Schrödinger's main ideas in relation to current science—clearing various persistent misunderstandings about how we should interpret their historical significance along the way—in order to assess how well they have stood the test of time (Sections 3 and 4). The third is to propose a new way of thinking about the impact that the book has had on the development of molecular biology (Section 5). And the fourth is to provide a novel account of what drove Schrödinger to write *What Is Life?* in the first place (Section 6).

To anticipate in a bit more detail what lies ahead, I will be arguing that Schrödinger's emphasis on the rigidity and specificity of the hereditary material (which stemmed from his attempt to explain biological order from physical principles) shaped how molecular biologists came to think about the structure and behaviour of macromolecules, resulting in a mechanical, deterministic, and genocentric view of the cell (and of development) that was instrumental in defining the agenda of molecular biology during the second half of the twentieth century. We will see, however, that cracks have begun to appear, as the shortcomings of this once-dominant view are becoming increasingly apparent. Regarding the genesis of *What Is Life?*, my contention shall be that Schrödinger turned to biology because he hoped that he would find in the molecular structure of living matter the means to salvage the mechanical and deterministic worldview of classical physics that he felt had become undermined by the orthodox Copenhagen interpretation of quantum mechanics. But more about that later.

My overarching aim is to help philosophers, historians, and biologists understand how we should read and think about this perennially popular book today, 80 years after its initial publication, and also to show that in the present context, *it really does matter* (even if one is utterly indifferent to history) what Schrödinger had to say about 'the physical aspect of the living cell' back in 1944. By systematically reconsidering the book's origins, argument, impact, and legacy, this Element aims to shed light on how molecular biology got to be where it is, and where it is likely to go next.

2 Reconstructing the Argument in *What Is Life*?

What Is Life? is a fairly short book—it is roughly as long as this Element. The first edition ran to 91 small pages. It is also accessible, with only five references to the technical literature and less than ten equations from start to finish. The prose is lively, with vivid imagery that often verges on the poetic (e.g., "if you are given a single radioactive atom, its probable lifetime is much less certain than that of a healthy sparrow" (Schrödinger 1944: 78)).

Despite all of this, the book does not make for easy reading. Stent (1966: 3) was right to point out that "though it seems to be clearly written, the clarity turns out to be deceptive", adding that "most readers must have had the uneasy feeling from time to time that perhaps they had not really understood what Schrödinger was trying to get across". Schrödinger himself acknowledges this on the very first page, stating that his Dublin audience "was warned at the outset that the subject-matter was a difficult one and that the lectures could not be termed popular" (Schrödinger 1944: 1).

My impression, however, is that what can make the book difficult to follow is not the subject matter per se, but the circuitous route that Schrödinger chooses to make his point, which reflects his own learning of the subject.[16] Accordingly, the book slides back and forth between speculations about the nature of the genetic material based on considerations of statistical mechanics and quantum theory on the one hand, and textbook-like expositions of Mendelian genetics coupled with reports of radiation-induced mutation experiments conducted on the fruit fly *Drosophila melanogaster* on the other. Schrödinger's central claims are

---

[16] Schrödinger is aware of the downsides of presenting matters in this roundabout way, and even sort of apologizes to the reader in advance: "I do not know whether my way of approach is really the best and simplest. But, in short, it was mine. [...] And I could not find any better or clearer way towards the goal than my own crooked one" (Schrödinger 1944: 4).

not presented in one go but are instead articulated piecemeal. There are also numerous physical, mathematical, and biological digressions—some important (such as the thermodynamic discussion of how the organism avoids succumbing to entropic decay), others considerably less so. In this section, I will reconstruct Schrödinger's line of reasoning as straightforwardly as possible and highlight the far-reaching implications that he draws from it.

Let us start with the title. Although the book is titled *What Is Life?*—an audacious choice that Sent (1966: 3) described as "a piece of colossal nerve"—Schrödinger does not address *that* question. The one that actually concerns him is less extravagant and more concrete, namely: *what is the nature of biological order?* The best way to approach the book, I think, is to regard it as Schrödinger's concerted attempt to answer *this* question.

As a physicist, Schrödinger begins by considering the kind of order described by physics. Chapter 1 is titled 'The Classical Physicist's Approach to the Subject'. Statistical mechanics teaches us that individual atoms are incapable of exhibiting orderly behaviour on their own because they are continuously subject to the disruptive stochastic effects of thermal agitation at any temperature above absolute zero. This is why most physical laws are *statistical*. Lawful regularities only emerge upon consideration of immense numbers of microscopic particles, which collectively display macroscopic patterns of order. Schrödinger refers to this as the *order-from-disorder principle*, and he takes it to be as fundamental in physics and chemistry as "the fact that organisms are composed of cells is in biology" (Schrödinger 1944: 9). He gives several examples to illustrate it.

One of them, depicted in Figure 4a, concerns what happens when you fill a glass vessel with fog—a visible aerosol of minute water droplets. Over time, the fog gradually sinks to the bottom with a well-defined velocity, determined by the viscosity of the air and the magnitude and specific gravity of the droplets. Still, if you observe one of the droplets under a microscope you find that it does not sink steadily with constant velocity but instead performs highly irregular movements, known as 'Brownian motion', as a consequence of thermal agitation. So, although the behaviour of any given droplet is random and disorderly as it sinks, the overall behaviour of the fog is regular and orderly. In general, the larger the number of participating particles in a physical process, the more precisely we can predict its behaviour. This is commonly referred to in statistics as the 'law of large numbers'.

A related example, shown in Figure 4b, is the familiar process of diffusion. If you add a small amount of a coloured substance—say, potassium permanganate—on one side of a vessel filled with water, over time it will spread evenly until it is uniformly distributed throughout the vessel. Notice that this is not due to any force driving the molecules away from the crowded region toward the less crowded one. It merely reflects the statistically predictable result of all permanganate molecules randomly being knocked about by the surrounding water molecules.

A third example, represented in Figure 4c, is the phenomenon of paramagnetism. A quartz tube filled with oxygen gas that is exposed to a magnetic field will result in the oxygen molecules orienting themselves parallel to the field, like a compass needle. But the molecules do not all turn in

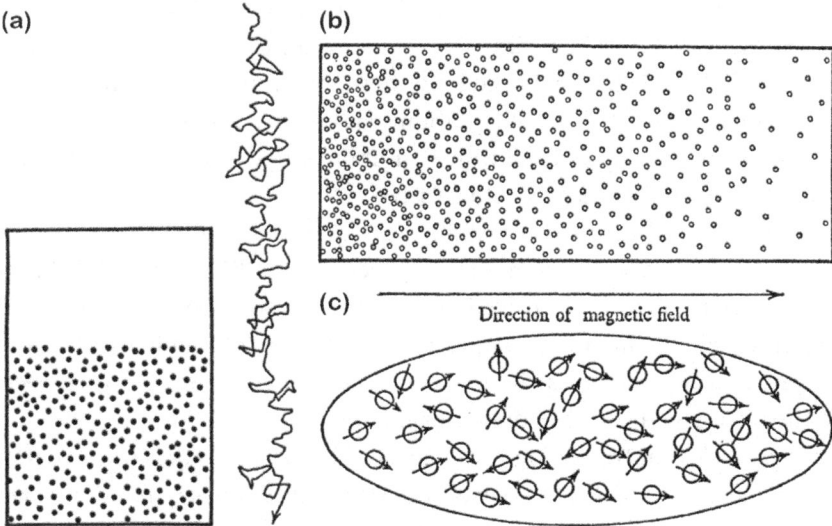

Figure 4 Schrödinger's illustrations of the order-from-disorder principle in *What Is Life?*. **(a)** The vessel on the left shows the regular sinking of fog over time. The downward arrow on the right delineates the irregular trajectory of an individual water droplet. The lawful behaviour of the fog reflects a statistical average of the combined behaviour of all its constituent droplets; **(b)** The concentration of the permanganate molecules in the vessel of water gradually decreases from left to right as the molecules diffuse until they are equally distributed. This orderly process is constituted by numerous 'random walks' performed by the permanganate molecules; **(c)** The oxygen molecules in the quartz tube, taken collectively, predictably align themselves with the magnetic field (adapted from Schrödinger 1944)

parallel at once. They keep changing their orientation incessantly due to thermal agitation. It is only because there is such a huge number of them that they appear on average to be aligned with the field.

Now, a "naïve physicist," Schrödinger writes, might be forgiven for supposing it to be obvious that the astonishing orderliness of an organism must likewise be based on the lawful macroscopic patterns of behaviour displayed by enormous ensembles of interacting molecules. But here comes the twist: "this expectation," he continues, "far from being trivial, is wrong" (ibid.: 18).

Schrödinger's reasoning is as follows. The order of an organism is "essentially determined" by its genes (ibid.: 20), and we know from experimental evidence that a gene molecule is not much larger than a million atoms. This number, he observes, "is much too small (from the [law of large numbers] point of view) to entail an orderly and lawful behaviour according to statistical physics" (ibid.: 30). Because genes are so tiny, they should not be able to reliably code for heritable traits, given that they are firmly in the grip of thermal agitation. And yet we know for a fact that genes *are* remarkably stable, "with a durability or permanence", he writes, "that borders upon the miraculous" (ibid.: 49).

Schrödinger illustrates this baffling predicament with the striking example of the 'Habsburg lip' (Figure 5), a genetic trait afflicting the Habsburg rulers that resulted in a protruding lower jaw, and which was faithfully preserved in this famous European family for many hundreds of years despite having a molecular basis and therefore being permanently subject to the relentless turbulence of thermal agitation.[17]

The puzzle that Schrödinger sets out to solve in the book is this: *how do we reconcile the small size of genes with their extraordinary stability in the face of constant stochastic perturbations?*

Given the inability of classical physics to account for the permanence of the gene, Schrödinger turns to the new quantum mechanics, in particular to the 1926–1927 Heitler–London theory of the chemical bond.[18] The interatomic forces postulated by this theory explain the crystalline

---

[17] Ernest Walton, a fellow Nobel laureate during Schrödinger's days at DIAS, recalled that around the time he was preparing his 'What Is Life?' lectures, Schrödinger told him he had inherited the shape of his nose from his grandfather, and that the gene responsible had somehow managed to remain stable for a century at more than 300° K (i.e., body temperature) (Pollard 1967: xi).

[18] Walter Heitler and Fritz London developed their theory in Zurich, where London had come to work with Schrödinger. Heitler later joined Schrödinger in Dublin and took over as director of DIAS when Schrödinger stepped down in 1946.

Figure 5 Portraits of members of the Habsburg dynasty across four centuries displaying the distinctive 'Habsburg Lip'. **(a)** Charles V, Holy Roman Emperor (1500–1558); **(b)** Rudolf II, Holy Roman Emperor (1552–1612); **(c)** Ferdinand II, Holy Roman Emperor (1578–1637); **(d)** Philip IV of Spain (1605–1665); **(e)** Leopold I, Holy Roman Emperor (1640–1705); **(f)** Charles II of Spain (1661–1700); **(g)** Archduke Charles, Duke of Teschen (1771–1847); **(h)** Archduke Albrecht, Duke of Teschen (1817–1895)

rigidity exhibited by solid matter. Schrödinger hypothesizes that the stability of the gene is afforded by the fact that its constituent atoms are also "bound together by those 'solidifying' Heitler–London forces" (ibid.: 60). The gene is a large molecule that is stable, he argues, because it "presents the same solidity of structure as a crystal" (ibid.).[19] However, unlike the ordinary crystals known to physicists, which display regular and periodic configurations, Schrödinger postulates that the structure of the gene must be nonrepetitive—or 'aperiodic'—in the sense that every atom, or group of atoms, plays an individual role that is not equivalent to (or interchangeable with) that of many of the others. He vividly exemplifies the contrast between periodic and aperiodic crystals by comparing it to the difference "between an ordinary wallpaper in which the same pattern is repeated again and again in regular periodicity and a master of embroidery, say a Raphael tapestry, which shows no dull repetition, but an elaborate, coherent, meaningful design traced by the great master" (ibid.: 3).

---

[19] Schrödinger even proposes the following correspondences: "molecule = solid = crystal" on the one hand, and "gas = liquid = amorphous" on the other (Schrödinger 1944: 59).

The reason the genetic material *must* be aperiodic, Schrödinger argues, is that only by exhibiting a nonrepetitive molecular structure could it possibly specify in such minute physical dimensions the detailed set of instructions required for the unfolding of ontogenic development. Schrödinger refers to this as the 'hereditary code-script', and he justifies its existence in the following terms:

> A well-ordered association of atoms, endowed with sufficient resistivity to keep its order permanently, appears to be the only conceivable material structure that offers a variety of possible ('isomeric') arrangements, sufficiently large to embody a complicated system of 'determinations' within a small spatial boundary. Indeed, the number of atoms in such a structure need not be very large to produce an almost unlimited number of possible arrangements. (Schrödinger 1944: 61)

Schrödinger illustrates this enormous number of possible specifications with the example of the Morse code, where only two signs, dot (·) and dash (—), are enough to codify the entire alphabet.[20] "[I]t is no longer inconceivable", Schrödinger concludes, "that the miniature code should precisely correspond with a highly complicated and specified plan of development and should somehow contain the means to put it into operation" (ibid.: 62).[21]

As Schrödinger sees it, then, "the mechanism of heredity is closely related to, nay, founded on, the very basis of quantum theory" (ibid.: 47). But quantum mechanics does not just come to the rescue in *What Is Life?* to safeguard the durability of the gene; Schrödinger also appeals to it to explain the relatively rare occurrence of genetic mutations. By likening the gene to a stable state of a quantum-mechanical system, he suggests that we can think of mutation as the spontaneous and discrete transition of the system to an alternative 'isomeric' configuration (i.e., one with the same atoms stably rearranged) through the surmounting of a steep energy threshold. A gene can thus be expected to occasionally 'jump' from one allele form to another, thereby increasing the heritable variation in a population in a way that can be potentially acted upon by natural selection.

Let us now turn to the last two chapters—in many ways the climax of the book—where Schrödinger articulates the main lesson he wishes

---

[20] The invocation of the Morse code in this context has led to a great deal of confusion about what Schrödinger meant by 'code-script'. We will examine this interpretive issue in Section 3.

[21] Later, when thinking about multicellular organisms, Schrödinger uses the metaphor of a "tiny central office" to refer to the hereditary material found in each of its constituent cells. He asks, rhetorically: "do they not resemble stations of local government dispersed through the body, communicating with each other with great ease, thanks to the code that is common to all of them?" (Schrödinger 1944: 79).

to draw from his detailed examination of genetics. Taking stock, he asserts that the "admirable regularity and orderliness" that characterizes the processes of life, which is "unrivalled by anything we meet with in inanimate matter", turns out—against the physicist's expectations—to be deterministically "controlled by a supremely well-ordered group of atoms" (ibid.: 77) specifying the hereditary code-script. These orderly biological processes, he writes, are "guided by a 'mechanism' entirely different from the 'probability mechanism' of physics" (ibid.: 79). Life is subject to what Schrödinger calls the *order-from-order principle*, which he explicitly contrasts with the order-from-disorder principle described at the start of the book (recall Figure 4).

In this crucial respect, organisms are analogous to machines, whose orderly and predictable operation is not a consequence of statistical regularities either but of the fact that they are constituted by solid-state structures large enough to remain unaffected by the stochastic perturbations of thermal agitation. To the extent that a piece of clockwork behaves mechanically, it is as if it operated at absolute zero. In the same way, the behaviour of organisms resembles "that purely mechanical (as contrasted with thermodynamical) conduct to which all systems tend, as the temperature approaches the absolute zero and the molecular disorder is removed" (ibid.: 69–70). Schrödinger thus arrives at his final "conclusion that the clue to the understanding of life is that it is based on a pure mechanism, a 'clock work'" (ibid.: 82) that "also hinges upon a solid—the aperiodic crystal forming the hereditary substance, largely withdrawn from the disorder of heat motion" (ibid.: 85).

Schrödinger anticipates that as further progress is made in the elucidation of the order-from-order hereditary mechanism—progress that he predicts will come not from further physical theorizing but from experimental work in "biochemistry under the guidance of physiology and genetics" (ibid.: 68)—we should expect to find *new laws of physics* operating in the organism: "living matter, while not eluding the 'laws of physics' as established up to date, is likely to involve 'other laws of physics' hitherto unknown" (ibid.: 68–69). This famous pronouncement, which Schrödinger notes "was my only motive for writing this book" (ibid.: 68), has frequently been misunderstood as implying a veiled defence of anti-reductionism in biology. However, a close reading of the text dispels this interpretation.

Schrödinger compares the present inability of the known laws of physics to fully account for the behaviour of an organism to the inability of an engineer who, knowing how a steam engine works, encounters an electric generator, such as a dynamo, for the first time. Both of these mechanical contraptions contain many of the same materials, but unless the engineer has studied electrical phenomena, he will be unable to understand the workings of the dynamo. Even so, Schrödinger adds, "[h]e will not suspect that the dynamo is driven by a ghost because it is set spinning by the turn of a switch, without furnace and steam" (ibid.: 76). Instead of concluding that the laws of physics break down when applied to the dynamo, the engineer will simply realize that he is being confronted with the behaviour of matter under a new set of conditions that he has not yet analyzed. Like the dynamo, the organism is just *a new kind of physicochemical machine*, governed by non-statistical, yet-to-be-discovered, order-from-order laws—laws, that is, that can explain how the microscopic order in the hereditary substance is amplified to produce the macroscopic order exhibited by the organism.[22]

Schrödinger makes an important digression from his main line of argument in the penultimate chapter to consider the bearing of the second law of thermodynamics on the organism, "forgetting at the moment all that is known about chromosomes, inheritance, and so on" (ibid.: 70). This well-known law negates the possibility of a perfectly efficient transformation of heat into work. It describes the irreversible tendency for the disorder in a system, measured in terms of *entropy*, to increase until the system reaches thermodynamic equilibrium. In a remarkably elegant discussion—undoubtedly one of the most memorable in the whole book—Schrödinger shows that there is no contradiction between nature's inexorable trend to become increasingly disordered (as mandated by the second law) and life's prodigious ability to preserve and propagate order (by means of reproduction). By eating, drinking, breathing, and so on, the organism imports the energy it needs to maintain its ordered state and thereby compensate for "all the entropy it cannot help producing while alive" (ibid.: 72). In other words, the organism eludes (at least for a time!) the inert state of thermodynamic equilibrium that we call 'death' by drawing into itself free energy from its surroundings—which Schrödinger refers to as 'negative entropy'. However, it is only able to do so at the expense of increasing the entropy (in the form of heat and other metabolic waste products) of the environment.

---

[22] Notice that when Schrödinger speaks of 'order *from* order', the contrast is not merely temporal or causal, but also spatial: *macroscopic* order is produced by, or arises from, *microscopic* order. The same is true when he speaks of 'order *from* disorder'.

Schrödinger does not go on to explain the "organism's astonishing gift of concentrating a 'stream of order' on itself and [...] of 'drinking orderliness' from a suitable environment", though he does note that this physiological capacity to maintain order "seems to be connected to the presence of the 'aperiodic solids', the chromosome molecules" (ibid.: 77).

What Is Life? ends with a five-page epilogue, 'On Determinism and Free Will', that had not been part of the original lectures. Schrödinger first notes that the physical processes taking place in the brain when one is thinking are "if not strictly deterministic at any rate statistico-deterministic" (ibid.: 87). Addressing the physicists in particular, he emphasizes that, "in my opinion, and contrary to the opinion upheld in some quarters, *quantum indeterminacy* plays no biologically relevant role in them" (ibid.). As I will show in Section 6, this is an extremely revealing statement, even though its significance has escaped the notice of almost all commentators of the book.

Finally, Schrödinger tries to reconcile two seemingly contradictory statements: "(i) My body functions as a pure mechanism according to the Laws of Nature" and "(ii) Yet I know, by incontrovertible direct experience, that I am directing its motions" (ibid.). He does so by retreating from science altogether and adopting the Vedanta metaphysical belief that individual consciousness is an illusion. We are all aspects of one single, omnipresent, eternal being—'Brahman', which is somewhat akin to God in the Judeo-Christian tradition. Hence Schrödinger's conclusion: "I am God Almighty", which, he is the first to admit, "sounds both blasphemous and lunatic" (ibid.: 88).

Most readers of *What Is Life?* were utterly baffled by the epilogue, to the extent that many chose to ignore it altogether. In his review of the book, Muller described it as a piece of "straight old-fashioned mysticism", adding that it is "startling to find it in a serious work by an otherwise so responsible scientist" (Muller 1946: 92). Haldane, for his part, wryly quipped that "[a] mechanist must either give a mechanistic account of mind, or turn a somersault. In his epilogue, Schrödinger does the latter with very great elegance" (Haldane 1945: 376).

3 A Critique of the Order-from-Order Principle

We begin now our appraisal of Schrödinger's argument in *What Is Life?* as it strikes the modern reader, starting with an examination of the order-from-order principle, which Schrödinger stresses is "the real clue to the understanding of life" (Schrödinger 1944: 82). This principle accounts for the transmission of biological order and locates it in the code-script that Schrödinger thinks is contained in the genes. A first question that the reader of *What Is Life?* might have is how original Schrödinger's ideas really are, so this seems as good a place as any to begin our analysis.

The most easily recognizable influence on *What Is Life?* is a 1935 German-language paper titled 'On the Nature of Gene Mutation and Gene Structure' co-authored by *Drosophila* geneticist Nikolai Timoféeff-Ressovsky, radiation physicist Karl Zimmer, and the aforementioned Delbrück (Timoféeff-Ressovsky et al. 1935, TZD hereafter), which Schrödinger alludes to several times in the book.[23] TZD is divided into four sections, one written by each co-author and a conclusion jointly written by the three. Schrödinger draws on the detailed review of gene mutation research that Timoféeff-Ressovsky provides in his section, and especially on the quantum-mechanical model of the gene and of mutation that Delbrück offers in his. Indeed, one of the chapters in *What Is Life?* is titled 'Delbrück's Model Discussed and Tested', where Schrödinger even declares that "[i]f the Delbrück picture should fail, we would have to give up further attempts" (Schrödinger 1944: 57). The notion that the gene is a well-defined material entity of a molecular order of magnitude, that it exhibits remarkable chemical stability, and that mutation can be construed in terms of stable rearrangements in its atomic structure, are all claims in *What Is Life?* that Schrödinger explicitly takes from TZD.

This has led some prominent commentators, such as embryologist and geneticist Conrad Hal Waddington, to go as far as to describe *What Is Life?* as "a re-writing of the classical paper which we used to refer to as TZD" (Waddington 1969: 321). Similarly, the famed structural chemist Max Perutz claimed that "the chief merit of *What Is Life?* is its popularization of [TZD] that would otherwise have remained unknown outside the circles of geneticists and radiation biologists" (Perutz 1987a: 558).

Still, if one pays closer attention to what Schrödinger argues than to whom he cites, it becomes clear that he owes a greater intellectual debt to Muller than to Delbrück in his thinking about genes and in his postulation of an order-from-order principle. Muller had begun working in Morgan's legendary 'fly room' at Columbia, and he was only the second geneticist to be awarded the Nobel Prize, after Morgan himself. By the early 1920s, Muller was passionately arguing—against most of his geneticist colleagues—that genes, far from being purely hypothetical units

---

[23] TZD was recently translated into English and republished alongside six historiographical commentaries in a splendid volume titled *Creating a Physical Biology: The Three-Man Paper and Early Molecular Biology* (Sloan and Fogel 2011).

conveniently postulated to account for inheritance patterns observed in crossbreeding experiments so as to make them amenable to mathematical treatment (see, e.g., Johannsen 1923), are in fact real "ultramicroscopic particles [...] [that] play a fundamental role in determining the nature of all cell substances, cell structures, and cell activities" (Muller 1922: 32). While most early geneticists, including Morgan, displayed a keen awareness of the complex relationship existing between genes and their developmental expression, Muller defended a far more reductionistic and deterministic view that afforded genes ontological and causal priority in the explanation of biological order.

Muller's views are perhaps most forcefully expressed in his manifesto 'The Gene as the Basis of Life' (1929), where he argues, inter alia, that genes are: (i) well-defined physical units composed of chain-like arrangements of elementary parts; (ii) capable of 'autocatalysis' in a process analogous to crystallization; and (iii) the primary agents responsible for the organism's morphological and physiological features. Schrödinger follows Muller in all these respects. He takes for granted that genes are "the most vital parts of an organism" (Schrödinger 1944: 2) and, in effect, "the material carrier[s] of life" (ibid.: 3). Also like Muller, Schrödinger suggests that genes are composed of long sequences of repeatable elements, and he uses the crystal analogy to explain their properties.

Muller even anticipated the need for physicists to get involved in the study of the gene. In a 1936 address to the Soviet Academy of Sciences titled 'Physics in the Attack on the Fundamental Problems of Genetics', Muller remarked that "genes have properties which are most unique from the standpoint of physics", and whose elucidation "may throw light not only on the most fundamental questions of biology, but even on fundamental questions of physics as well" (Muller 1937: 210). Muller closed his address by calling on physicists to join him in examining these "ultimate particles of life itself" (ibid.), proclaiming that "[t]he geneticist himself is helpless to analyze [them] further. Here the physicist [...] must step in. Who will volunteer to do so?" (ibid.: 214). Eight years later, Schrödinger took on precisely this challenge in *What Is Life?*, though at no point does he discuss or even cite Muller's work.[24] I shall have much more to say about Delbrück and TZD, as well as about Muller, in Section 6.

---

[24] Muller was clearly aware of the striking similarities between Schrödinger's views and his own. In his review of *What Is Life?*, Muller accepts with resignation that Schrödinger, "having become acquainted with [the problems of genetics] from the reading of a relatively limited group of publications, [...] appears unfamiliar with how far back most of them go in the thinking of biologists" (Muller 1946: 92). But his review of Schrödinger's

The suggestive notion of an order-from-order principle guiding the operation of the organism, then, is not Schrödinger's own invention, but rather reflects the bold genocentric views of several early-twentieth-century geneticists, especially Muller. The belief that there is a rigid, unchanging, static structure inside the body that determines its form and function precedes even the advent of genetics. It is implicit in the writings of several late-nineteenth-century biologists, most notably August Weissman (1893), who famously demarcated what he called the 'germ-plasm' from the rest of the body (or 'soma'), and who considered the former not just the bearer of inheritance but the central directing agency in control of development.

What Schrödinger contributes to the order-from-order principle—aside from making it explicit and deriving its necessity from purely physical considerations—is the groundbreaking idea of a hereditary *code-script*. This marks the introduction of the term 'code' into genetics, which, of course, proved to be an extremely fruitful metaphor. The extraordinary thing about Schrödinger's proposal is that it precedes the widespread adoption of information-talk in biology. Indeed, it arrives not only a decade before the discovery of the double helix, but even before DNA was conclusively identified as the hereditary substance (the crucial experimental demonstration by Oswald Avery, Colin MacLeod, and Maclyn McCarty was published the same year as *What Is Life?*).[25]

One of the most common claims made about the historical significance of *What Is Life?* is that Schrödinger's code-script was the forerunner of the *genetic code*—the quasi-universal set of rules by which nucleic acid base sequences are 'translated' into the amino acid sequences that make up proteins. The race to 'crack' the genetic code (recounted in Cobb 2015; see also Kay 2000) was one of the most dramatic events in molecular biology during the period immediately following the discovery of the double helix. (The code was not completely deciphered until 1966.)

Despite the frequency with which this attribution is made (e.g., Symonds 1986; Pauling 1987; Moore 1989; Sarkar 1991; Kauffman 1995;

---

book was positive overall, despite the detectable hint of sarcasm in the title of his review, 'A Physicist Stands Amazed at Genetics', and, of course, his aforementioned frustration with the epilogue. Recalling his 1936 plea to physicists, Muller bitterly remarks that "[i]f the collaboration of the physicist in the attack on biological questions finally leads to his concluding that 'I am God Almighty', and that the ancient Hindus were on the right track after all, his help should become suspect" (ibid.).

[25] In accordance with the views of leading geneticists of the time, such as Haldane and Darlington, Schrödinger speculates that the hereditary substance "is probably a large protein molecule" (Schrödinger 1944: 30).

Hendrickson 2011; Gribbin 2013; Sarkar 2013; Sigmund 2019), a careful reading of *What Is Life?* suggests that it is based on a misunderstanding of what Schrödinger means by 'code-script'. This is due to the unfortunate ambiguity inherent in the word 'code'. Often, this word is used to mean a *cipher*, that is, a system for exchanging one set of characters with another. The Morse code is an example, as it provides a standardized method for replacing the letters in the alphabet with dots and dashes. The genetic code is also a cipher, as it refers to the correspondence rules that specify how triplets of nucleotide bases (or 'codons') can be translated to amino acids.

However, the word 'code' can be used in a way that does *not* involve the translation of a message. It can refer instead to any system or collection of rules or instructions. Think of the highway code, or the Napoleonic code, or a code of conduct. This appears to be closer to what Schrödinger has in mind when he speaks of a hereditary code-script: a complex set of instructions that stipulates the nature and timing of the processes by which cells function and multicellular organisms develop. Notice that while the genetic code concerns only the relation between nucleic acids and proteins, the scope of Schrödinger's code-script extends far beyond that, "involving all the future development of the organism" (Schrödinger 1944: 61).

The reason this has not been generally acknowledged is that Schrödinger himself, as we saw in Section 2, resorts to the Morse code—a cipher—when describing his code-script. It is important to remember, though, that he does so *only to illustrate its combinatorial richness*. Schrödinger's point is that "an almost unlimited number" (ibid.) of distinct developmental determinations are possible if the relatively short association of atoms composing the code-script are arranged in different permutations (just as in the Morse code, only two signs in combinations of four or less are more than sufficient to specify all 26 letters of the alphabet). At no point when discussing his code-script does Schrödinger refer to (or imply the existence of) specific one-to-one correspondence rules between two sets of sequences, or two kinds of substances, which is what a cipher—like the genetic code—essentially involves.[26]

---

[26] The ever-astute Crick seems to have been aware of the potential for confusion on this issue, as the following snippet of Judson's recorded conversation with him indicates: ""[in naming the genetic code] we ought to have used the word 'cipher'," Crick said. I said that Schrödinger had first made the comparison with the Morse code. "Yes, that's right," Crick said. "And of course we all knew about that; so maybe we just took it over—but that's a mistake too: it should be Morse *cipher*."" (Judson 1979: 278)

This important interpretive point has been made recently by several commentators (Kay 2000: 61–62, Kogge 2012: 627–631, and especially Walsby and Hodge 2017). I agree with their analysis, but I think it does not go far enough. Not only is Schrödinger's code-script a rule-code for development rather than a cypher; I believe that we should regard it as the direct precursor to a biological concept that has proven to be almost as influential as the genetic code, namely the *genetic program*. Proposed 17 years after the publication of *What Is Life?* by Jacob and Monod (1961)—and simultaneously by evolutionary biologist Ernst Mayr (1961)—the genetic program "has come to be widely regarded as a fundamental explanatory concept for biological development" (Keller 2000: 74). "It equates the genetic material of the egg with the magnetic tape of a computer" (Jacob 1973: 9), and it is considered to play "a decisive role in laying down the structure of an organism, its development, its functions, and its activities" (Mayr 1997: 123). According to this notion, the fertilized egg is assumed to contain a program (akin to a computer program) that directs and controls the developmental process by executing a predetermined set of operations according to algorithmic instructions encoded in its genome.

While the genetic program enjoyed a great deal of popularity during the latter half of the past century, in recent decades it has become increasingly apparent that it fails to provide an adequate understanding of development. Much has been written about the conceptual inconsistencies and empirical inaccuracies of the genetic program (see, e.g., Newman 1988; Nijhout 1990; Lewontin 2000; Longo and Tendero 2007; Walsh 2020). I myself have argued in earlier work (i.e., Nicholson 2014) that the genetic program serves to legitimize three deeply problematic theses concerning the role of genes in development, namely:

1. *Neo-preformationism*: genes fully specify the outcome of development.
2. *Developmental computability*: complete knowledge of how genes interact during development should enable us to 'compute' the embryo.
3. *Genetic animism*: genes initiate, direct, and control development.

In what follows, I want to emphasize the remarkable extent to which Schrödinger's code-script prefigures the concept of the genetic program by showing how the descriptions that Schrödinger offers of it in *What Is Life?* already imply an unequivocal commitment to all of these theses.

Let us start with *neo-preformationism*. Preformationism refers to the ancient belief that the structure of the adult organism is already present in miniature form as a 'homunculus' encased in either the egg or the sperm, and that development simply consists in the mechanical enlargement of that structure. Today's neo-preformationism is more subtle: "the organism is not pre-formed in the head of the sperm, but the head of the sperm and the egg nucleus do carry an immensely complex, species-specific, regulatory program for the stepwise process of embryonic development" (Davidson 2009: R217). What development amounts to, in the words of Medawar (1965: 1329), is "an unfolding of pre-existing capabilities, an acting-out of genetically encoded instructions". The genome is thus assumed to contain all the information required to specify the organism. Neo-preformationism appears to have provided an important impetus for the Human Genome Project. One of its leading advocates, Nobel laureate Walter Gilbert, memorably declared that the "[t]hree billion bases [of a human's DNA] sequence can be put on a single compact disk (CD), and [in the future] one will be able to pull a CD out of one's pocket and say, 'Here is a human being; it's me!'" (Gilbert 1992: 96)

Now, if we look at the passage in *What Is Life?* where the term 'code-script' is first introduced, we find that Schrödinger does so in order to defend neo-preformationism. He begins by discussing "the four-dimensional pattern" of the organism, by which he means "the whole of its ontogenetic development from the fertilized egg cell to the stage of maturity" (Schrödinger 1944: 20). He observes that "this whole four-dimensional pattern is known to be determined by the structure of that one cell, the fertilized egg", specifically by the chromosomes in its nucleus. "It is these chromosomes", Schrödinger continues, "that contain in some kind of code-script the entire pattern of the individual's future development and of its functioning in the mature state" (ibid.). He expresses the same idea later, when he asks himself "how this tiny speck of material, the nucleus of the fertilized egg, could contain an elaborate code-script involving all the future development of the organism" (ibid.: 61).

Let us move on to *developmental computability*, which articulates the deterministic expectation that an embryo can in principle be computed from the complete data set of a fertilized egg. The question is this: "given a total description of the fertilized egg—the total DNA sequence and the location of all proteins and RNA—could one predict how the embryo will develop?" (Wolpert 1994: 270).[27] If the fertilized egg contains a program, then development must involve the predictable execution of an algorithmic succession of predetermined steps. The prospect of 'computing the embryo'

---

[27] Despite its modern overtones, developmental computability is actually a very old idea. In his embryological writings, René Descartes conjectured that "if one had a good knowledge of all the parts of the seed of some species of a particular animal, man for example, one could deduce from this alone, by entirely certain and mathematical arguments, every shape and structure of each of its bodily parts" (Descartes 1998: 200).

is probably most closely associated with Wolpert, who began exploring it in the 1970s (e.g., Wolpert and Lewis 1975). His hope was that by deciphering the commands coded in the program, it might be possible to uncover the precise sequence of developmental steps without becoming hopelessly entangled in all the messy molecular and cellular details of the process. Brenner pursued a similar research program during the same period (see de Chadarevian 1998).[28]

Looking back at *What Is Life?*, it is striking to find Schrödinger endorsing developmental computability so emphatically—and dramatically—in one of the most famous passages in the whole book, where he invokes the unforgettable image of the Laplacian demon to describe the deterministic character of his code-script:

> In calling the structure of the chromosome fibres a code-script we mean that the all-penetrating mind, once conceived by Laplace, to which every causal connection lay immediately open, could tell from their structure whether the egg would develop, under suitable conditions, into a black cock or into a speckled hen, into a fly or a maize plant, a rhododendron, a beetle, a mouse or a woman. (Schrödinger 1944: 20–21)

Finally, let us consider *genetic animism*. This is the belief that DNA exerts executive control over the organism's operations. It reflects the tendency to ascribe causal powers to genes, and to regard them not just as the material carriers of heredity, but as the primary agents of life. It is manifested when developmental geneticists speak of 'master control genes' (e.g., Gehring 1988) and it is a recurring theme in popular science books, such as Richard Dawkins' bestseller *The Selfish Gene* (1976). Genetic animism stems from what Evelyn Fox Keller has called the 'discourse of gene action', which characterized the thinking of some early American geneticists like Muller, for whom the cell is "only a by-product, originally, of the action of the gene material" (Muller 1929: 918). Keller herself puts it best: "Part physicist's atom and part Platonic soul, [the gene] was assumed capable simultaneously of animating the organism and of directing (as well as enacting) its construction" (Keller 2000: 47).

Schrödinger speaks of genes in exactly this way in *What Is Life?*. He states that they "play a *dominating* role in the very orderly and lawful events within a living organism. They have *control* of the observable large-scale features which the organism acquires in the course of its development, [and] they *determine* important characteristics of its

---

[28] For a philosophical defense of developmental computability, see Rosenberg 1997.

functioning" (Schrödinger 1944: 19, my emphasis). He also attributes agency to the code-script, noting that "the code-script must itself be the operative factor bringing about the development" (ibid.: 62). Indeed, he recognizes (in another famous passage) that

> the term code-script is, of course, too narrow. The chromosome structures are at the same time instrumental in bringing about the development they foreshadow. They are *law-code* and *executive power*—or, to use another simile, they are *architect's plan* and *builder's craft*—in one. (Schrödinger 1944: 21, my emphasis)

Sometimes, Schrödinger expresses more than one of the three theses in a single sentence, such as when he notes that "the miniature code should precisely correspond with a highly complicated and specified plan of development [*neo-preformationism*] and should somehow contain the means to put it into operation [*genetic animism*]" (ibid.: 62). It is difficult not to be reminded of such passages when reading Jacob and Monod's introduction of the genetic program concept 17 years later, when they conclude—clearly echoing Schrödinger—that "the genome contains not only a series of blue-prints [*neo-preformationism*], but a co-ordinated program of protein synthesis and the means of controlling its execution [*genetic animism*]" (Jacob and Monod 1961: 354).

Today, these three theses are perceived as seriously misguided by a growing number of biologists—not to mention philosophers of biology (see, e.g., Oyama et al. 2001). There are good reasons for this. The information required to specify an organism does not come preformed in the DNA. It emerges progressively through the interaction of DNA with other cellular components, as well as with the environment. Development is not the gradual unfolding of the organism from a prespecified genetic plan. It is a highly dynamic and heterogeneous process of construction involving the confluence of numerous interacting causal factors, only some of which have their basis in the DNA.

Similarly, developmental computability is an illusion. Gene expression—like any molecular process—is subject to stochastic fluctuations. Developmental 'instructions' reflect probabilistic tendencies, not deterministic mandates. The goal to 'compute the embryo' is irreconcilable with the fundamentally stochastic character of the molecular and cellular processes that underlie development. We will return to this point in Section 4.

Lastly, genetic animism attributes a causal agency to genes that they simply do not possess on their own. It is difficult to see how genes could possibly be responsible for initiating, directing, and controlling development, given that DNA is not an inherently active molecule, but rather requires activation from without. By itself, DNA is inert, relatively unstructured, and non-functional. To be functional, it needs to be embedded in an already organized, living cell. Despite what is often claimed, genes are not 'self-replicating'. Nor do they 'make' proteins, or 'switch on' molecular pathways. All these processes require the orchestrated involvement of many other molecules inside the cell, especially proteins. In other words, it is only in the presence of the highly structured cellular environment that any talk of 'gene action' even makes sense.

Crucially, it is not just the function of genes that is a product of the cellular context, but also their *stability*. This is the real key to solving the puzzle that lies at the heart of *What Is Life?*. Schrödinger was undoubtedly perceptive in reasoning that the material substratum of the code-script would need to be bound together by the same covalent bonds that make crystals so stable. The DNA double helix is indeed stabilized by long chains of phosphodiester covalent bonds linking the external sugar–phosphate strands of the helix, as well as by the hydrogen bonds connecting the complementary pairs of nucleotide bases inside the helix (three in the case of cytosine and guanine, two in the case of adenine and thymine). But the stunningly reliable transmission of order during reproduction that we observe in the perpetuation of genetic traits like the Habsburg lip (recall Figure 5) is *not* primarily a consequence of the crystal-like stability of the DNA molecule.

The reason the replication, transcription, and translation of genetic information is so astonishingly accurate is that there is an entire army of proteins in the cell whose job it is to proofread and correct any errors accrued during these processes.[29] It is not that genes behave as if they were at absolute zero; genetic processes are as susceptible to thermal agitation as anything else! It is just that the cell devotes a considerable amount of its energetic resources to minimizing the disruptive effects of stochasticity. Genes do not impose stability on the cell; it is rather the other way round. To put it another way, the stability that so deeply impressed Schrödinger is not an intrinsic property of the structure of the genetic material, but *a continuous accomplishment of the cell operating as a whole*.

Summing up, what should we make of the order-from-order principle in light of current knowledge? In one sense, Schrödinger was right to suppose that

---

[29] For example, the ability of DNA polymerases to select correct nucleotides and excise mistakenly incorporated ones during DNA replication reduces the error rate from 1 in 10^4 bases to about 1 in 10^9. (For a recent review, see Bębenek and Ziuzia-Graczyk 2018.)

there is a "stream of order" (Schrödinger 1944: 77) transmitted from parent to offspring, and that it is intimately connected to the hereditary substance. It is also the case that this substance has an aperiodic atomic structure—exactly as Schrödinger predicted—that allows it to store inordinate amounts of data, which helps account for the amazing diversity of organisms. There is even a code-script of sorts after all, as the genome does specify the amino acid constitution of the proteins that carry out most functions in the cell.

On the other hand, Schrödinger was wrong to assume that the code-script determines all of the organism's observable characteristics (i.e., its phenotype). This mistake was compounded by the molecular biologists who derived the idea of the genetic program from his code-script, as they took genes to provide not just instructions to synthesize proteins, but a blueprint to make an organism. The phenotype cannot be read from the information stored in the genes. Genetic information acts only as a resource for development, not as a step-by-step guide. It only acquires meaning in the context of the cell and of the external environment. Schrödinger was also wrong to endow genes with legislative and executive powers. DNA does nothing alone. It is the whole cell that acts. Even the stability of genes is an achievement of a coordinated set of subcellular processes—which is what a molecular biologist today would answer if asked about the puzzle that troubled Schrödinger in *What Is Life?*.

Finally, we now know that the order transmitted in reproduction is not exclusively encoded in the DNA. Although the amino acid sequence of proteins derives from DNA, protein function is primarily determined by cellular context (Kupiec 2010; Nicholson 2019). Moreover, many subcellular compartments and structures, such as membrane-bound organelles, as well as the plasma membrane itself, serve as templates for their own replication—they are the only source of 'information' for their own regeneration. Proteins do get incorporated into them, but they are always already formed and thus constitute distinct and irreducible repositories of cellular order.[30] It is a mistake to think of the information encoded in the DNA as the only thing that gets transmitted from parent to offspring. Membranes and organelles, basal bodies and microtubule organizing centres, are all inherited as well. These channels of epigenetic inheritance have been the subject of much recent research (see Jablonka and Lamb 2014; Bondiuransky and Day 2018). Rudolf Virchow was right when he

---

[30] Moss makes a lucid and compelling case for taking these membrane-based cellular compartmentalizations seriously as non-genetic instances of order-from-order in chapter 3 of his book *What Genes Can't Do* (2003).

memorably declared in the mid nineteenth century that *it takes a cell to make a cell*. None of the cell's constituents, *including DNA*, is the sole basis of the order it exhibits. As Moss (2003: 91) has aptly put it, "Schrödinger's order-from-order descriptor well characterizes the cell as a whole—but only as a whole".

4 A Critique of the Order-from-Disorder Principle

The other key principle that Schrödinger discusses in *What Is Life?*—indeed, the one he starts with—is the order-from-disorder principle. It is to this notion that we now turn. As we saw in Section 2, this principle describes how predictable patterns of orderly behaviour emerge when a large number of entities is considered collectively, even if the composing entities, taken individually, display no order whatsoever. Schrödinger discusses and even graphically illustrates several examples of order-from-disorder phenomena in the first chapter of *What Is Life?*, three of which are reproduced in Figure 4. This principle is the foundation upon which the edifice of statistical mechanics is built. Let us briefly review the origins of this field, as this will help us understand the significance of the principle.

The rise of statistical thinking in the nineteenth century led to a profound transformation in our understanding of nature (see Porter 1986). Chance, which had previously been regarded as a sign of our ignorance of causal relations, became 'tamed'—to use Ian Hacking's (1990) suggestive phrase—when it was realized that robust statistical regularities could be identified in large data sets. Even in the absence of causal knowledge, it became possible to make reliable predictions using the language of probability. Initially, the adoption of the statistical method in physics was a matter of practical convenience. When James Clerk Maxwell developed the kinetic theory of gases—which explains the macroscopic properties of gases (e.g., volume, pressure, temperature) in terms of the positions and velocities of their constituent microscopic particles—the application of statistics allowed billions of gas particles to be treated as a single ensemble, thereby avoiding the utterly impractical task of having to calculate the trajectory of each individual particle. It was later realized, however, that even if it *were* possible to track the trajectory of every particle, this would not tell us anything that we could not already surmise from a statistical treatment of the ensemble as a whole. In the statistical mechanics of Boltzmann and J. Willard Gibbs, it is the behaviour of the *collective*, rather than that of any given individual, that is of interest. The fact that statistics focuses on populations at the expense of ignoring individuals came to be regarded as a strength rather than a limitation. For these physicists, statistics was no longer a convenient methodological tool; it had become an indispensable explanatory resource.

A sublime illustration of this is Boltzmann's statistical explanation of the second law of thermodynamics. Confronted with the problem of reconciling the irreversible trend for the entropy in a system to increase (a phenomenon later described by Arthur Eddington as the 'arrow of time') with the reversible nature of the mechanical interactions of the microscopic particles in that system, Boltzmann showed that this inevitable entropic increase reflects only a *statistical tendency* for the system to move towards more probable, and more disordered, microscopic arrangements. To put it another way, the observed directionality of macroscopic processes that the second law prescribes arises from the expected statistical behaviour of the ensemble of microscopic particles over time. The law therefore expresses a *probability*, not an absolute certainty—though, given the astronomical number of particles typically involved (recall the law of large numbers discussed in Section 2), it is a probability that can safely be regarded as a certainty for all practical purposes.

By the early twentieth century, it had become clear that the lawful regularities observed for many physical and chemical phenomena were similarly statistical—all following the same order-from-disorder principle discussed in the first chapter of *What Is Life?*.[31] Towards the end of the book, Schrödinger poetically describes this principle as "our beautiful statistical theory of which we [physicists and chemists] were so justly proud because it allowed us to look behind the curtain, to watch the magnificent order of exact physical law coming forth from atomic and molecular disorder" (Schrödinger 1944: 80).

Nevertheless, we should not forget that one of the main theses in *What Is Life?* is that the order-from-disorder principle, despite its overwhelming importance in physics and chemistry, is *irrelevant* to the explanation of biological order. As Schrödinger asserts at the start of the book, "it is in relation to the statistical point of view that the structure of the vital parts of living organisms differs so entirely from that of any piece of matter that we physicists and chemists have ever handled physically in our laboratories or mentally at our writing desks" (ibid.: 2–3). In this section, I will examine this contention. We will see that a compelling case can be made,

---

[31] Statistical order-from-disorder regularities do not just reign over physics and chemistry. They can be found in many other natural and social sciences, including meteorology, geology, geography, sociology, economics, and history.

contra Schrödinger, that the order-from-disorder principle is as central to explanations in biology as it is to explanations in physics.

The simplest way to make this case is to point to Charles Darwin's theory of evolution, which notably deals with *populations*, as opposed to individuals. No individual ever evolves; it is rather the population, considered over many generations, that is subject to evolutionary change. The activities of individual organisms may be disorderly or unpredictable, but as long as there is heritable variation in the population that leads to differences in reproductive success among its members, then evolution by natural selection (an order-producing process if there ever was one!) will inevitably follow (Lewontin 1970).[32] Modern evolutionary biology is statistical through and through. In fact, the triumvirate credited with supplying the mathematical foundation of evolutionary theory, namely Francis Galton, Karl Pearson, and R. A. Fisher, contributed as much to the establishment of mathematical statistics as to the theory of evolution. Indeed, they viewed the two as inseparable (Pence 2022).[33] In evolutionary biology, just as in statistical mechanics, collective patterns of order can be reliably predicted despite—or rather, *because* of—the unpredictable nature of individual events. As Fisher paradoxically put it, "[t]he effects of chance are the most accurately calculable, and therefore the least doubtful, of all the factors of an evolutionary situation" (quoted in Porter 1986: 319).[34]

Population genetics and evolutionary biology are not outliers. Order-from-disorder phenomena are studied in other fields that deal with the dynamics of biological populations, such as ecology, where the Lotka-Volterra predator-prey equations are sometimes compared to the ideal gas law in physics (e.g., O'Dwyer 2020), or ethology, where collective animal behaviours—like the trajectories of flocking birds—are routinely investigated using models drawn from statistical mechanics (e.g., Bialek et al. 2012). Thus, it is simply not true that the order-from-disorder principle plays no role in the living world.

But perhaps we are being uncharitable to Schrödinger. After all, *What Is Life?* is concerned with the order displayed by an *individual* cell, or

---

[32] Given Darwin's appeal to order-from-disorder reasoning, it is not surprising to learn that Boltzmann himself stated in 1886 that the nineteenth century would one day be remembered as "the century [...] of Darwin" (Boltzmann 1974: 15).

[33] Something else this illustrious trio had in common was their enthusiastic promotion of eugenics (see Mackenzie 1981).

[34] Like Schrödinger, Fisher was a great admirer of Boltzmann (Hodge 1992; Depew and Weber 1995: chap. 10). In fact, his celebrated 'fundamental theorem of natural selection' was explicitly modelled after Boltzmann's statistical reformulation of the second law of thermodynamics (see Fisher 1930: 36–37).

organism, not by a population. Can Schrödinger's claim be maintained if it is understood in this more restricted way? On the face of it, if we consider a single cell, Schrödinger cannot be faulted for downplaying the order-from-disorder principle. We now know that most functionally important macromolecules in the cell exist in such minuscule quantities that the law of large numbers does not apply to them.[35] As a result, the internal architecture of the cell must impose constraints on where specific individual molecules find themselves at any given time in order to maximize the probability that they will interact in a way that ensures that all cellular functions are carried out appropriately and in a timely fashion (see Nicholson 2019).

The most dramatic example is the DNA molecule in a bacterial cell, of which there is usually only one copy, and yet the cell's survival depends on the information in this one molecule being appropriately replicated, transcribed, and translated in a timely fashion by an array of other molecules. Note, though, that replication, transcription, and translation are just as probabilistic as any other sequence of chemical reactions. Indeed, the stochastic character of gene expression accounts for why there is so much variation between genetically identical cells—the reason being that the molecular processes that underlie them, owing to thermal agitation, never occur in exactly the same way or take precisely the same time.[36]

The cell, then, appears to make do without relying on order-from-disorder regularities. What about the multicellular organism? Recall that Schrödinger introduces his hereditary code-script idea not merely, or even primarily, to account for the order exhibited by the cell, but to explain the formidably complex multicellular process of *development*. We already saw in Section 3 that the genetic program model, which I suggested is the direct successor to Schrödinger's code-script, faces numerous problems. Do order-from-disorder approaches to development fare any better?

Despite the preponderance of preformationist, order-from-order reasoning in the history of embryology, the process of development is actually quite amenable to a characterization in terms of statistical mechanics (see, e.g., García-Ojalvo and Martínez Arias 2012). The spatiotemporal

---
[35] The conditions in a cell are, of course, very different from the conditions in a test tube preparation, which typically does contain high concentrations of the pertinent molecules and where it is therefore possible to make reliable statistical predictions.
[36] This non-genetic heterogeneity is often referred to as 'noise'—a term borrowed from engineering that is rather misleading in molecular biology (see Nicholson 2020). Far from disruptive, this noise plays a key role in many cellular processes (Huang 2009; Eldar and Elowitz 2010).

organization of the developing embryo requires highly coordinated sequences of cellular differentiation events. These events result from 'decisions' made by individual cells about their fate, which are in turn prompted by the expression of certain genes. Although these cell fate decisions are intrinsically stochastic and are not reproducible on an individual basis, they nevertheless result in highly regular—almost deterministic—spatiotemporal patterns at the level of the whole ensemble of cells (the embryo). In other words, *order* at the macroscopic scale (i.e., the reliable generation of tissues and organs) predictably arises out of *disorder* at the microscopic scale (i.e., the noisy molecular process of gene expression). It is possible in principle, then, to understand development as an order-from-disorder phenomenon.

What makes statistical mechanics so appealing as a theory is that it provides a systematic way of connecting the macroscopic properties of a system to its microscopic constituents. Interestingly, this has become one of the chief goals of developmental biology: to establish links between events at the molecular (or microscopic) scale and those at the multicellular (or macroscopic) one. And researchers are increasingly looking to the conceptual resources of statistical mechanics to aid them in this task. For instance, Boltzmann's aforementioned confrontation with the entropic arrow of time is clearly being evoked when researchers emphasize the need "to explain the 'arrow of time' in gene expression dynamics" (Teschendorff and Feiberg 2021: 461). This refers to the challenge of accounting for the *macroscopic directionality* of gene expression patterns as cells progressively differentiate to form distinct tissues given the *microscopic reversibility* of the activation and repression of the individual genes involved. Another example is the suggestion that pluripotency is a statistical property of stem cell populations that typically arises out of highly variable molecular microstates (see MacArthur and Lemischka 2013).

A useful way of comparing order-from-order and order-from-disorder accounts of development is to consider their respective stances on determinism. Schrödinger's code-script, and the genetic program that arose from it, takes the developmental process to be determined all the way down to the molecular level. The obvious determinacy of development at the macroscopic level (i.e., the fact that the journey from fertilized egg to adult organism reliably follows a well-defined series of morphological stages that results in an essentially predictable outcome) is seen as a direct consequence of the deterministic action of genes, which are assumed to contain a detailed blueprint for development, or at least a complex set of algorithmic instructions for its programmatic execution.

In contrast, order-from-disorder models of development do not infer determinism at the microscopic scale on the basis of the observed determinacy at the macroscopic scale. This point was perceptively made half a century ago by the organicist developmental theorist Paul Weiss (1973), who illustrated it in a memorable diagram, redrawn in Figure 6. Weiss pointed out that the preservation of topographic relations during two successive stages of development allows us to experimentally identify regions of an early embryo as being the predictably earmarked forerunners for the formation of specific organs (e.g., heart, brain, liver, kidneys). Nevertheless, such clear-cut correlations between stages do not hold at the cellular level (and even less so at the molecular level). That is, if we follow the differentiation trajectories of particular cells in these prospective organ areas from the earlier to the later period, we find them taking far more fortuitous routes, differing individually from case to case. Thus, although

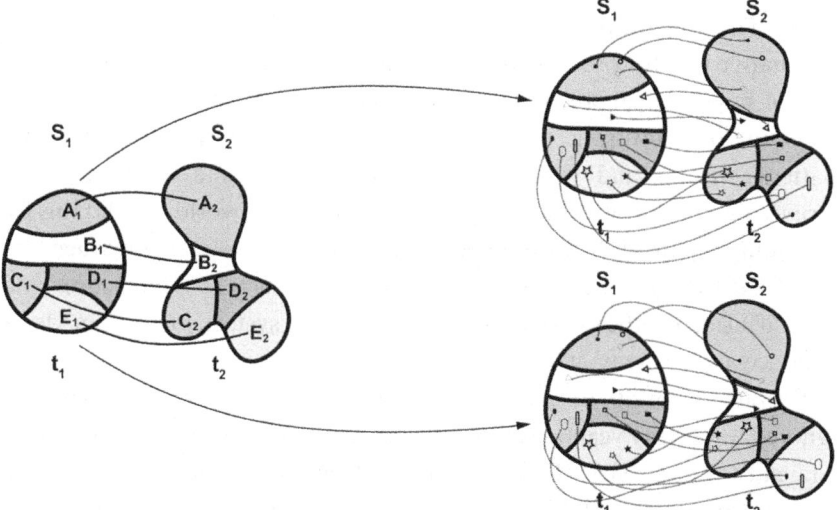

Figure 6 Schematic depiction of the persistence of the topographic pattern of whole embryonic regions despite a lack of regularity in the positions of their constituent cells. The left side shows the *macroscopic view* of the regions of an embryo between developmental stages S_1 and S_2. At t_2, every embryonic region (A_2, B_2, C_2, D_2, E_2) can be traced back to a corresponding region (A_1, B_1, C_1, D_1, E_1) at t_1. Yet if we take a *microscopic view* of the same process, shown on the right side, we find that even two very closely related embryos (top and bottom) exhibit a great deal of variation in the precise trajectories undertaken by their cells (depicted as symbols) in each embryonic region (based on Weiss 1973)

the coarse-grained development of organ rudiments can be mapped out in a precisely determinable fashion, the fine-grained molecular and cellular processes that underlie it, *when considered individually*, remain indeterminate and unpredictable. Macroscopic order, in this model, far from being the mechanical amplification of an underlying microscopic order, arises in the system *despite* the indeterminate and disorderly activities of the individual microscopic elements. Weiss himself pithily described the resulting situation as "determinacy in the gross despite demonstrable indeterminacy in the small" (ibid.: 21–22).[37]

The case for understanding development as an order-from-disorder phenomenon can be strengthened further by broadening our conception of the order-from-disorder principle itself. So far, we have taken Schrödinger's own formulation of the principle at face value, as we have assumed that linear statistical effects are the only way of getting order out of disorder. But we now know that this is not so. Eight years after *What Is Life?* appeared, the mathematician Alan Turing published a landmark paper titled 'The Chemical Basis of Morphogenesis' (1952) that suggested an alternative way for order to arise from disorder. Turing showed that a system of hypothetical chemical substances (which he called 'morphogens') reacting and diffusing together can spontaneously produce periodic patterns—peaks and valleys of concentration—in the form of spots, stripes, or spirals not unlike those found in the living world. He did this by providing a pair of differential equations and demonstrating mathematically that by adjusting the relevant parameters (such as the reaction rate and diffusion coefficient of each morphogen) the system could be made to produce a wide array of spatial patterns.

Despite its novelty (or perhaps because of it), Turing's paper was all but ignored for twenty years, save for a few exceptions (e.g., Waddington 1962; Maynard Smith 1968). However, in 1972 mathematical biologists Hans Meinhardt and Alfred Gierer revived Turing's 'reaction–diffusion model' and showed that a system of two interacting morphogens—specifically, a slow-diffusing activator coupled with a fast-diffusing inhibitor—could in principle account for the basic properties of biological patterning processes (Gierer and Meinhardt 1972). Since then, numerous kinds of stable

---

[37] Of course, a great deal of progress has been made in experimentally mapping out developmental cell fates since Weiss's time. For simple multicellular organisms like the tiny nematode worm *Caenorhabditis elegans*, we are even able to precisely track the lineage of all 671 of its embryonic cells (Sulston et al. 1983). However, such perfectly predictable behaviour is absent in most other developmental systems given the greater compounding effect of stochastic fluctuations.

biological patterns have been successfully recreated in computer simulations using variations of this model, including the spiral arrangement of leaves on a plant stem (a phenomenon called 'phyllotaxis'), the distribution of feather buds, and the pigmentation patterns of mollusc shells (Kondo and Miura 2010; Ball 2015). Perhaps the most impressive reaction–diffusion computer models are those that faithfully replicate the characteristic markings on the fur coat of feline predators and the elaborate stripe patterns of tropical fish, examples of which are shown in Figure 7a and 7b.[38]

Still, the striking resemblance of these computer simulations to the real patterns displayed by organisms does not by itself establish that Turing-style reaction–diffusion systems are causally responsible for them. In fact, the experimental identification of diffusing activator and inhibitor morphogens has proven elusive. Turing's theory suffered a serious blow early on when it was discovered that the stripe-like

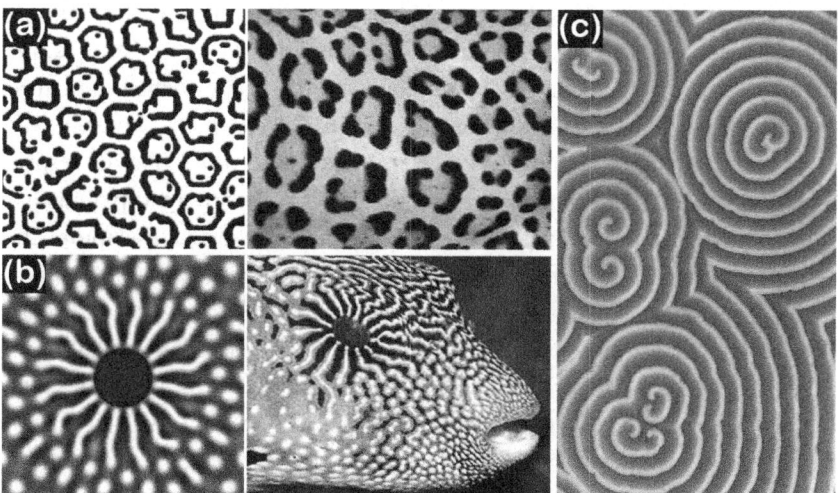

Figure 7 Examples of kinds of order-from-disorder processes not considered by Schrödinger in *What Is Life?*. **(a)** Reaction–diffusion simulation of the 'rosette' markings of a jaguar (adapted from Ball 2015); **(b)** Reaction–diffusion simulation of the radial stripe patterns of the map pufferfish *Arothron mappa* (adapted from Kondo and Miura 2010); **(c)** Patterns consisting of travelling waves of chemical concentrations produced by a Belousov–Zhabotinsky reaction in a petri dish (Credit: David Maitland)

---

[38] Readers can explore for themselves the boundless possibilities opened up by reaction–diffusion models by trying out one of the various interactive simulation tools freely available online; see, for example, https://pmneila.github.io/jsexp/grayscott/.

patterns in the early *Drosophila* embryo are not produced by an elegant reaction–diffusion system (as had been conjectured by some of the theory's earliest advocates) but instead results from the sequential activation of an unwieldy cascade of genes according to a gradient of mRNA molecules laid down in the egg prior to fertilization (Akam 1989). This important finding, which earned its discoverers the Nobel Prize in 1995, suggested that at least some aspects of *Drosophila* development are best approached from a conventional order-from-order perspective.[39] In turn, this made most developmental biologists skeptical of the idea that reaction–diffusion systems are genuinely involved in biological pattern formation. As a result, Turing's theory in biology has remained, until very recently, nothing more than a tantalizing hypothesis—a possible explanation awaiting empirical confirmation (cf. Harrison 1987; Keller 2002: chap. 3; Maini 2004).

The situation has changed dramatically in the last fifteen years, as real-life Turing-style morphogens have now been identified for a considerable number of developmental phenomena.[40] To mention just one example, the regularly spaced ridges in the mammalian mouth palate (which are called 'rugae') appear to be the product of a reaction–diffusion system involving the proteins fibroblast growth factor and Sonic hedgehog, which operate respectively as activator and inhibitor. Nevertheless, it is becoming apparent that Turing's original model is probably too simple to realistically capture the actual dynamics of patterning processes during morphogenesis (a possibility that Turing already contemplated in his 1952 paper). Although the existence of reaction–diffusion systems is no longer in doubt, it is likely that most developmental patterns are produced not by simple activator–inhibitor pairs, but by more complex systems involving three or more factors—perhaps in combination with the activation of gene regulatory networks.[41]

Be that as it may, the key lesson for us here is that Turing's model provides precisely what Schrödinger thought was inconceivable: a means of producing order during development in the absence of a pre-existing genetic template (i.e., a code-script). As Ball has aptly observed, "Turing seems to have identified one of nature's general mechanisms for generating order

---

[39] It is quite ironic that Turing would end up proposing an order-from-disorder model of development, given that the order-from-order model it competes with is based on a metaphor—the genetic program—that owes its existence, by virtue of being grounded in the modern computer, to Turing's own foundational work in this area.

[40] For a recent progress report on research in this area, see the thematic issue 'Recent progress and open frontiers in Turing's theory of morphogenesis', published in 2021 in volume 379, issue 2213 of *Philosophical Transactions of the Royal Society A*.

[41] A thoughtful attempt to combine these ideas can be found in Green and Sharpe 2015.

from macroscopic uniformity and microscopic disorder" (Ball 2015: 9). Notice that this order-from-disorder mechanism is totally different from the one that Schrödinger speaks so fondly about in *What Is Life?*, as its physical foundation is not late-nineteenth-century statistical mechanics but mid-twentieth-century *non-equilibrium thermodynamics*. Indeed, as it turns out, 'Turing patterns' are but one example of a much larger set of order-from-disorder phenomena that can be brought together under the banner of *self-organization*.[42]

Around the time that Turing was developing his theory, the Soviet chemist Boris Belousov used a mixture of reagents to create oscillating patterns in vitro, which were further explored by Anatoly Zhabotinsky in the 1960s. The so-called 'Belousov–Zhabotinsky reaction' (Figure 7c), became one of the first well-understood instances of chemical self-organization. The connections between these travelling waves and Turing's stationary patterns began to emerge shortly thereafter in the pioneering work of Ilya Prigogine and his group at the Free University of Brussels, who named them 'dissipative structures' because they are sustained by the dissipation of energy in a non-equilibrium process. Dissipative structures are everywhere. Familiar examples include candle flames, whirlpools, and tornadoes. Prigogine's greatest achievement (for which he was awarded the Nobel Prize in 1977) was to show how self-organization arises in nature—that is, to explain how the macroscopic patterns of order displayed by dissipative structures arise spontaneously from non-linear molecular interactions and become dynamically stabilized in far-from-equilibrium conditions through an ongoing flux of energy and matter (see Nicolis and Prigogine 1977; Prigogine and Stengers 1984).

The crucial biological significance of these developments is that *organisms themselves* are also dissipative structures—albeit of a vastly more complex kind than any of the aforementioned examples. Thermodynamically speaking, a cell is a membrane-bound open system (open, that is, to the flow of both energy and matter) that maintains itself in an irreversible, low-entropic 'steady state' far from equilibrium.[43] Not only is the cell as a whole a dissipative structure, but research in the last couple of decades has confirmed that many subcellular assemblies (including the mitotic spindle, the Golgi apparatus, and the nucleolus) are highly dynamic steady-state

---

[42] The concept of self-organization—introduced by Immanuel Kant in his third critique to distinguish organisms from machines—has a long and convoluted history that I cannot review here. For an excellent overview, see Keller 2008, 2009.

[43] I have examined the philosophical implications of understanding organisms as dissipative structures in Nicholson 2018.

systems capable of spontaneously self-organizing into morphologically and functionally distinct configurations through intrinsically stochastic interactions (Kirschner et al. 2000; Karsenti 2008; see also Nicholson 2019).[44]

Empirical findings of this kind serve as powerful reminders that the 'information' that specifies the cell's spatiotemporal organization is not wholly encoded in the genome. It is highly misleading to speak of a genetic blueprint for the cellular architecture when we know that so much of it is generated by self-organization in the absence of an external template or a global plan. Of course, this is not to say that genes are not important; it is only to assert that they do not causally bring about the spatiotemporal organization of the cell, as is implied by the idea of a code-script or a program. Instead, gene products are released into a cellular milieu that is *always already structured*, and they exert their influence under the physical constraints of the existing four-dimensional order—much of which is shaped and reconstituted by ongoing self-organizing processes.

It is time to take stock of what our analysis in this section has revealed. The order-from-disorder principle, as Schrödinger understands it, is as indispensable to biology as it is to physics. Statistical mechanics is indeed founded on it, but so is modern evolutionary biology. Recent research suggests that it is likely to become indispensable in developmental biology as well, and not just because of the problems and limitations of competing order-from-order models. In addition, it is clear in hindsight that Schrödinger's construal of the order-from-disorder principle in terms of linear statistical regularities is overly restrictive, as there are other ways in which order can emerge from disorder in nature, most notably by self-organizing processes. Today, we know that such processes are crucial not just for pattern-formation during morphogenesis (as Turing predicted), but more fundamentally for the generation and maintenance of the cell's internal architecture.

We can conclude, then, that life is a manifestation of order-from-order *and* order-from-disorder processes. The former are necessary for its propagation, but the latter play a key role in its conservation. Both are essential for its perpetuation over longer (evolutionary) time scales.

In Section 5, we will turn our attention to the historical reception of *What Is Life?* and challenge the assessment that professional historians

---

[44] Besides self-organization, yet another 'non-classical' way in which order can arise from disorder is by the coordinated coupling of stochastic processes. A fascinating example inside the cell is the Brownian ratchet mechanism for directed movement that is thought to be employed by some motor proteins. I have examined this order-from-disorder process in detail elsewhere; see Nicholson 2019: 116–119 and Nicholson 2020: 55–58.

have given of the book's role in the development of molecular biology. Before doing so, however, it is necessary to dispel some persistent misconceptions about the legacy of Schrödinger's book in discussions of self-organization and non-equilibrium thermodynamics, as these are topics that we have addressed in this section.

One of the most surprising things about the way *What Is Life?* is discussed today is that it is often described as a foundational document in biological thermodynamics—despite the fact that, as we saw in Section 2, Schrödinger only discusses thermodynamics as an aside in the penultimate chapter to point out that metabolism is what keeps the organism from succumbing to entropic decay. Although Schrödinger never uses terms such as 'self-organization', 'steady state', 'open system', or 'far-from-equilibrium conditions', it is possible to read him, with the benefit of hindsight, as having anticipated certain features of dissipative structures (as Prigogine would later call them). If this was all that was claimed, there would hardly be a need to even mention it. But many contemporary advocates of non-equilibrium thermodynamics go much further, and in the process, they do serious violence to the facts.

Their first mistake is to credit Schrödinger with identifying and resolving the conflict between life's propensity towards order and the inexorable increase in disorder mandated by the second law of thermodynamics. Although Schrödinger explains away the apparent contradiction lucidly and concisely in *What Is Life?*, he was certainly not the first to do so. The tension between life and the second law was identified almost a century earlier by the founders of thermodynamics, particularly Hermann Helmholtz and Lord Kelvin. Thereafter, various late-nineteenth-century authors tried to elucidate the peculiar kinds of stability exhibited by organisms. Herbert Spencer spoke of a 'moving equilibrium', Gustav Fechner of a 'tendency toward approximate stability', Emil Du-Bois Reymond of a 'dynamic balance', and so on. Already by the 1920s and 1930s, biochemists were describing the thermodynamics of living systems in recognizably modern terms.[45] Donnan, who as I indicated in Section 1 was one of Schrödinger's most important influences, wrote about the topic in 1928 in terms that clearly foreshadow the famous remarks we find in *What Is Life?*:

> [L]iving beings, just like inanimate things, conform to the second law [of thermodynamics]. They do not live and act in an environment which is in perfect physical and chemical equilibrium. It is the non-equilibrium, the free or available energy, of the environment which is the sole source

---

[45] Keller 2008 provides a characteristically enlightening discussion of this history; see also Nicholson 2018.

of their life and activity. [...] [A]n animal lives and acts because its food and oxygen are not in equilibrium. [...] [E]quilibrium is death. (Donnan 1928: 1559)

The second mistake that biological thermodynamicists make is to anachronistically project back the modern meaning of order-from-disorder as self-organization onto Schrödinger's Boltzmannian conception of order-from-disorder, thereby occluding the vital role played by statistical mechanics in *What Is Life?*. Again, although Schrödinger does discuss how the organism takes in energy and matter from its surroundings as a means of evading entropic decay, the possibility of organization spontaneously emerging in far-from-equilibrium conditions—that is, of order-from-disorder in the modern sense of non-equilibrium thermodynamics—does not even occur to him. At any rate, it is a notion that runs directly counter to what Schrödinger is arguing for in his book.[46]

But the misinterpretations of *What Is Life?* go deeper still. Recent commentators have claimed that Schrödinger argues that the order-from-disorder principle is just as central to the explanation of life as the order-from-order principle (e.g., Hendrickson 2011; Sigmund 2019), or that he answers the question 'What is life?' twice, first using his order-from-order principle and then using his order-from-disorder principle (e.g., Walsh 2015), or—perhaps most bizarrely of all—that he prophetically envisioned two research programs for future biology: one based on his order-from-order principle (which resulted in molecular biology) and another based on his order-from-disorder principle (which resulted in non-equilibrium thermodynamics) (e.g., Murphy and O'Neill 1995; Hendrickson 2011).

One can find all of the above misconceptions in the writings of the ecological thermodynamicist Eric Schneider. Schneider brands the tension between life and the second law 'The Schrödinger Paradox', falsely claiming that "Schrödinger was the first to emphasize the need to grapple with life from a thermodynamic perspective" (Schneider and Sagan 2005: 16).[47] He declares anachronistically that Schrödinger "proposed that to study living systems from a nonequilibrium perspective would reconcile

---

[46] I am not the first to notice this. Here is how Moss (2003: 61) expresses the same observation: "The idea of dynamic self-organization [...] is exactly what Schrödinger denies. Indeed, it is just because the seat of biotic order must thereby be secured through its removal from the heat flux of the cell and, owing to its inertness, its exclusion from the biotic dynamics of the cell, that its characterization as a code-script presents itself as apropos".

[47] This attribution not only flies in the face of the historical record, but it also obscures the fact that, as we saw in Section 2, Schrödinger already has a very different paradox on his hands in *What Is Life?*, namely the question of how to reconcile the molecular size of genes with their miraculous stability in the face of stochastic perturbations.

biological self-organization and thermodynamics" (Schneider and Kay 1994: 26), and even that Schrödinger "expected that such a study would yield new principles of physics" (ibid.)—thereby misinterpreting the oft-quoted remark about 'new laws of physics' we discussed in Section 2. He also mistakenly takes Schrödinger to be arguing that "life was comprised of two fundamental processes; one 'order from order' and the other 'order from disorder'" (ibid.: 25) and that these principles "outlined two future sciences: the molecular biology that has proved to be such a force in the world, and the thermodynamics of biology that has yet to prove its mettle" (Schneider and Sagan 2005: 7–8).

It seems that Schneider himself is responsible for fabricating and spreading these myths about *What Is Life?*. Their first appearance in the literature is in a brief letter that Schneider wrote to *Nature* in 1987 (i.e., Schneider 1987). One does not find them in any of the earlier works devoted to biological thermodynamics (e.g., Morotwitz 1970; Dyson 1985; Wicken 1987). When *What Is Life?* is mentioned in these earlier treatments of the subject, it is generally in a *critical* vein to point out that Schrödinger overestimated the importance of his order-from-order principle. Before Schneider, nobody appears to have conflated Schrödinger's Boltzmannian order-from-disorder principle with the Prigoginian notion of self-organization, as commentators today so frequently do. In fact, Prigogine went out of his way to avoid this precise confusion, declaring that he "introduced the term 'dissipative structures' to contrast such structures from the equilibrium structures [...] based on Boltzmann's order[-from-disorder] principle" (Nicolis and Prigogine 1977: 4) and that he prefers to "call this order 'order through fluctuations' to contrast it with the Boltzmann order[-from-disorder] principle" (ibid.: 5).[48]

So why have Schneider and others gone to so much trouble to artificially inflate the importance of *What Is Life?* for the development of biological thermodynamics? The answer, I think, is obvious. Schrödinger is, after all, one of the most revered physicists of the twentieth century—a veritable "deity of science", in Schneider's own words (Schneider and

---

[48] Even before Prigogine's 'order through fluctuations', the Viennese polymath Heinz von Foerster had already recognized in 1960 the need to distinguish self-organization, and what he termed 'order from noise', from what Schrödinger had called 'order from disorder' in *What Is Life?*: "reading recently through Schrödinger's booklet I wondered how [...] his keen eyes escaped [...] a 'second clue' to the understanding of life, or—if it is fair to say—of self-organizing systems. Although the principle I have in mind may, at first glance, be mistaken for Schrödinger's 'order from disorder' principle, it has in fact nothing in common with it. Hence, in order to stress the difference between the two, I shall call the principle I am going to introduce to you presently the 'order from noise' principle" (von Foerster 1960: 43).

Sagan 2005: 12). To be able to claim him as the founder of your discipline is to bestow a considerable amount of respectability on what you are doing. Moreover, if the spectacular successes of molecular biology can be plausibly interpreted as the process of working out the implications of Schrödinger's order-from-order principle, then, provided that you grant yourself the license to liberally reconstruct his order-from-disorder principle so that it refers to self-organization (as opposed to the regularities described by statistical mechanics), you can triumphantly proclaim without much fear of embarassment that "[p]erhaps fifty years from now *What Is Life?* will be seen as prophetic for its treatment of the thermodynamics of living systems rather than for the prediction of the structure of the gene" (Murphy and O'Neill 1995: 3). This is exactly what Schneider means when he "advocate[s] flipping over Schrödinger's record and listening to its other side" (Schneider and Sagan 2005: 24).

But enough about thermodynamics. Let us return now, without further delay, to the more famous first side of 'Schrödinger's record'.

5 Rethinking Schrödinger's Impact on Molecular Biology

Despite the problematic appropriation of *What Is Life?* as a foundational document in biological thermodynamics, most readers might reasonably assume—given the wealth of evidence presented in Section 1—that the book's reputation as a cornerstone of molecular biology remains firmly secured. In fact, the opposite is the case. Surprisingly, perhaps, a consensus of sorts has emerged among historians of science that Schrödinger's book actually had little discernible impact on the rise of molecular biology, and that its importance for the field was recognized only *retrospectively* by its foremost practitioners. Historians have drawn attention to the fact that the bombastic declarations of influence collected in Box 1 were all made *after* the establishment of molecular biology (Wilkins was the first to do so in his Nobel Lecture of 1962, and others followed shortly thereafter), and that such flamboyant pronouncements were really nothing more than thinly veiled self-serving attempts to confer an aura of epistemic prestige on the new biology of the post-war period by conveniently associating it with the intellectual authority of one of the greatest physicists of the twentieth century.[49]

---

[49] In a sense, these historians have accused the pioneers of molecular biology of doing the same thing I have accused Schneider of doing in the context of non-equilibrium thermodynamics—and for the same reasons.

Pnina Abir-Am was one of the first to 'deconstruct' these autobiographical attributions of influence by leading molecular biologists as "efforts to gain legitimacy as the proponents of a new scientific ultra-discipline" (Abir-Am 1985: 104) and as attempts to "define their own history while 'proving' their affiliation to a hero-scientist, thereof projected as an ancestor of molecular biology" (ibid.: 113). Abir-Am identifies three reasons for the persistent appeals to Schrödinger's *What Is Life?*. First, as a founder of quantum mechanics—a discipline that had radically transformed physics some decades earlier—Schrödinger was perceived as a respectable revolutionary, which is precisely the image that molecular biologists sought to convey of their own field: revolutionary (to help attract newcomers) yet respectable (to gain institutional acceptance as an autonomous new area of research and teaching). Second, Schrödinger's intrepid theorizing from physical principles and his apparent lack of concern with chemical details exemplified the new approach to biology that molecular biologists hoped to promote. And third, since Schrödinger was no longer alive, it was "safe to invoke him as a real ancestor, i.e., part of a cult of the notable dead, [as] he could not interfere or reply that he neither anticipated molecular biology nor took an interest in it" (ibid.: 104).

Others have made similar claims. Lily Kay (2000: 59) discusses how the pronouncements in Box 1 "serve to buttress this 'founding father' narrative", thereby "reinforcing the canonization process". Leah Ceccarelli (2001: 65) writes that the molecular biologists making those pronouncements were jumping on the "*ex post facto* bandwagon" by "draw[ing] on the authority of a text that would rationalize their professional choices to others" (ibid.: 66). And Keller (1990: 404) remarks that "Schrödinger's legacy [in molecular biology] depended so little on the utility of any of his particular biological arguments, and so much on disciplinary politics".

In effect, what these historiographical analyses suggest is that *What Is Life?* had already lost its topicality as a 'scientific object' by the 1950s, and "by the 1960s the molecular biologists were looking back with nostalgia to a 'historical object'" (Witkowski 1986: 267). It is this "later decontextualization and reinvention of *What Is Life?* [that] enhanced its prescience and durability" (Kay 2000: 61), allowing it, only in retrospect, to "become the stuff of prophecy" (ibid.: 62)—a science classic that molecular biologists "mostly read for reassurance" (Rosen 1996: 168).

We are told that autobiographical declarations of influence so long after the fact cannot be trusted, as "it is virtually impossible to believe most of what one is told about things that happened 30 to 40 years ago" (Symonds

1986: 224). And even if *What Is Life?* did inspire some to take up the molecular study of life, "the impact of Schrödinger's views on biological matters has been, in the strictly scientific sense, negligible" (Dowdle 1989: 104). His book cannot "be said to have provided any actual suggestions for further research that proved to be useful" (Keller 1990: 403).

The negative tenor of these modern assessments has been fuelled to a considerable degree by the surprisingly disparaging remarks of the two Nobel laureates who were asked to reappraise *What Is Life?* on the occasion of Schrödinger's centennial (Kilmister 1987), namely Linus Pauling and Perutz. Pauling, who briefly worked under Schrödinger in 1927, first makes the point that given the extent to which molecular biology is indebted to principles of modern chemistry that are themselves founded on quantum mechanics (such as the Heitler–London theory of the covalent bond discussed in Section 2), we are justified in asserting that "Schrödinger, by formulating his wave equation, is basically responsible for modern biology" (Pauling 1987: 228). However, his evaluation is drastically different when it comes to *What Is Life?*. "When I first read this book, over 40 years ago", he writes, "I was disappointed. It was, and still is, my opinion that Schrödinger made no contribution to our understanding of life" (ibid.: 229). Pauling's criticisms focus on the book's brief treatment of thermodynamics, which he considers "vague and superficial to an extent that should not be tolerated even in a popular lecture" (ibid.).[50] He particularly chastises Schrödinger for speaking confusingly of 'negative entropy' instead of employing the more theoretically appropriate concept of free energy, and he contemptuously declares that by coining this nonsensical notion, *What Is Life?* "made a negative contribution" to biology (ibid.).[51]

Perutz, for his part, admonishes Schrödinger for, among other things, his outdated presentation of genetics, his failure to recognize key theoretical

---

[50] It is, of course, delightfully ironic that the section of *What Is Life?* that advocates of non-equilibrium thermodynamics (and many others) have found most illuminating and inspiring is the very same section that Pauling—arguably the greatest chemist of the twentieth century—finds most wrongheaded and infuriating.

[51] Pauling's complaints are similar to those put to Schrödinger in 1946 by another distinguished chemist, his former Oxford colleague Francis Simon. In response to his exchange with Simon, Schrödinger appended a two-page addendum to the thermodynamics chapter in the book's second edition of 1948 (which has been retained in all subsequent reprintings) to justify his introduction of the term 'negative entropy'. He admits that if he had only been addressing physicists (as opposed to a general audience), he would have stuck to the less colourful, yet more technically precise, concept of free energy. But he also mentions a precedent set by Boltzmann, who already contemplated the bearing on life of 'entropy taken with a negative sign' (the remark is found in an address that Boltzmann gave in 1886; see Boltzmann 1974: 24).

insights known at the time (such as George Beadle and Edward Tatum's 'one gene–one enzyme hypothesis', published in 1941), and his ignorance of chemistry, which helps resolve the apparent contradiction between the stability of the gene and the statistical laws of physics. Perutz's (1987b: 243) caustic conclusion is that "a close study of his book and of the related literature has shown me that what was true in his book was not original, and most of what was original was known not to be true even when the book was written". Perutz also lambasted *What Is Life?* in a commentary in *Nature* (i.e., Perutz 1987a), as well as in a brief note in the April 5 1987 issue of *The Scientist*, which he scornfully titled '*What Is Life?* Fiction, Not Science'.[52]

I suspect that the virulence of these remarks, which contemporary historians have gleefully quoted when giving their damning verdicts on the book's scientific value, goes some way towards explaining the puzzle with which I started this Element—the question of why, despite the book's enduring fame and classic status, there has been so little appetite among recent scholars to engage seriously with Schrödinger's argument, beyond paying lip service to the three soundbites listed in Section 1.

Now, the historians have been absolutely right to draw attention to the strategic ways in which prominent molecular biologists in the 1960s started deploying Schrödinger's reputation to validate their own interests and endeavours. But it is important not to overstate the case to the point where the impression conveyed is that it took twenty years for molecular biologists to start paying attention to *What Is Life?*. There is actually plenty of evidence to the contrary, some of which was already adduced in Section 1, including the recently unearthed letter that Crick sent to Schrödinger just weeks after the publication of the double helix model of DNA in 1953 (recall Figure 3). Yet even the more moderately revisionist reappraisals that do acknowledge that Schrödinger's book was widely read when it came out but maintain that its chief importance does not lie on what it said, or even on how it was said, but rather on who said it, are still problematic. In this section, I will argue—against the prevailing historiographical consensus—that the ideas Schrödinger advanced in *What Is Life?* (and to a lesser extent, also the way he chose to present them) did in fact exert a

---

[52] It is interesting to contrast Perutz's derogatory remarks with the edifying ones made two decades earlier by his close collaborator and fellow Nobel laureate John Kendrew (1967: 141), who asserted that "Schrödinger's *What Is Life?* [...] had an enormous influence, particularly on physical scientists, in altering fundamental outlooks on biology, and in encouraging the new way of approaching the study of living organisms that has come to be known as molecular biology".

considerable influence in shaping and consolidating the research agenda of molecular biology during the second half of the twentieth century.

As we saw in Sections 2 and 3, Schrödinger's central thesis is that the source of all cellular order (and, by implication, all organismic order) resides in the code-script embedded in the fixed, solid-state structure of the genetic material, which protects it from the randomizing effects of thermal agitation. Now, Schrödinger does not tell us *how* the order in the aperiodic crystal is used or relayed so that the cell can perform its operations in an orderly way. He anticipates that the "detailed information about the function of the genetical mechanism" will emerge not from physics but from further experimental studies in "biochemistry under the guidance of physiology and genetics" (Schrödinger 1944: 68). What he *does* tell us is that this future research will disclose, as Moss (2003: 60) carefully words it, "new higher-level laws or principles that explain the ability of living systems to parlay high levels of order between the chemically stable but metabolically inert aperiodic crystal and the growing and metabolizing, but entropically vulnerable, apparatus of the cell and organism".

One of the principal claims I want to propose in what follows is that Schrodinger's vision of the cell as a microscopic machine operating deterministically according to non-statistical, mechanical principles—and thereby impervious to the disruptive effects of stochasticity—provided a tacit conceptual framework for molecular biology within which empirical results could be interpreted, as well as a direction towards which further research could be oriented. It is in this context, I believe, that we should understand Schrödinger's famous quip about "[n]ew laws to be expected in the organism" (Schrödinger 1944: 76). What he had in mind was laws (or principles, or mechanisms) that would account for the genocentric, order-from-order logic that he predicted would soon be discovered operating at the heart of the cell.

I begin by emphasizing what I take to be a crucial implication of Schrödinger's argument, namely that in the absence of statistical regularities, the order encoded in the structure of the aperiodic crystal must somehow be reliably transmitted to other cellular components, especially to the *proteins*, so that these can individually express it through their respective functions in a way that similarly eludes or overcomes the raging Brownian storm of the molecular realm. This Schrödingerian understanding of cellular order as the summative result of the order of its separate macromolecules is, I would argue, part of what makes molecular biology so different from the older biochemical tradition that preceded it, which had assumed the cell to be a homogeneous solution or colloidal suspension—a sort of 'bag of chemicals'—governed by the statistical, order-from-disorder laws of chemical kinetics. Richard Lewontin expounds this point in a remarkably crisp passage that deserves to be quoted in full:

> In *What Is Life?* Schrödinger pointed out that the mechanism of inheritance required the seemingly contradictory attributes of extremely high precision of a chemical mechanism and very low concentrations of molecules. That is, the molecular mechanism of heredity must be based not on the Laws of Mass Action, on statistical properties of ensembles of molecules, but on the individually repeatable behavior of separate molecules. This behavior is a result of the structure of the molecules themselves rather than the thermodynamic properties of their milieu. The entire process of reproduction in turn must be explained in terms of a chain of molecular events in proper temporal order and with the molecules occupying specific sites or moving in specific pathways. Always the emphasis is on individual molecules in space and time rather than ensembles averaged over space and time. Molecular biology, unlike classical biochemistry, places the emphasis on discreteness rather than continuity, on deterministic rather than average statistical behavior. (Lewontin 1968: 160)

This composite (as opposed to systemic) conception of cellular order, with its emphasis on the *specific* structure of *individual* molecules, which interact with one another *mechanically* and *predictably*, is exactly what one finds in the writings of the pioneers of molecular biology. Jacob and Monod express it clearly in their influential 1961 paper in which the genetic program concept is introduced when they describe the genome as "a mosaic of independent molecular blue-prints for the building of individual cellular constituents" (Jacob and Monod 1961: 354). It is also apparent in the way proteins are characterized as miniature machine tools. It is the reason why Perutz calls haemoglobin a "molecular lung" and "an organ on a molecular scale" (quoted in Judson 1979: 213), and why Medawar asserts that "[t]here is no dividing line between structures in the molecular and in the anatomical sense" (ibid.). As Judson remarks, for molecular biologists, "genetical events, like biochemical ones, now really felt as though they were rightly explained only when they could be conceived mechanically, in terms of the pieces and links and angles and local electrical charges that molecules are made of" (ibid.: 215–216).[53]

---

[53] A few sentences earlier, Judson offers a vivid description of the replacement of biochemistry's colloidal conception of cellular order by molecular biology's structural and mechanical conception: "when enormous molecules with fixed structures emerged from the colloidal slime and seized the positions of power in the cell, DNA the dictator ordering its protein soldiers, the previous concerns of biochemists were subsumed as intermediate processes" (Judson 1979: 215).

In noting molecular biology's exaltation of molecular structure, it is worth saying something about one of the key ideas in *What Is Life?*, namely the concept of an *aperiodic crystal*. A number of commentators have been baffled by Schrödinger's unorthodox use of the word 'crystal' to describe the genetic material. Waddington (1969: 321) described it as "an exceedingly paradoxical phrase". Some have wondered why he did not resort to a more suitable chemical term, such as 'macromolecule' or 'polymer'. Both Crick (in Judson 1979: 245) and Perutz (1987b: 241) take this odd terminological choice as evidence that Schrödinger had little understanding of chemistry. However, a very different interpretation suggests itself when we recall why Schrödinger invokes the idea of a crystal in the first place, which is that he is trying to solve the paradox of the permanence of the gene by appealing only to *physical* principles, especially the Heitler–London theory derived from quantum mechanics, which accounts for the structural stability of molecules and of solid matter.

As I indicated in Section 2, it is by virtue of the 'solidifying' interatomic forces described by this theory that Schrödinger concludes that the hereditary substance *must* be a large molecule exhibiting the solid-state rigidity of a crystal. Notice that Schrödinger arrives at this conclusion completely independently of any chemical considerations about genes. For this reason, Robert Olby (1974: 242) has suggested—plausibly, in my view—that "Schrödinger deliberately avoided using chemical evidence". By accounting for the stability and mutability of genes in quantum-mechanical terms, "Schrödinger made the facts of genetics meaningful to the physicist", so that "a physicist reading this book could get excited about genetics" (ibid.: 245). If Olby is right, then the way Schrödinger chose to make his case *really did* make a difference to the physicists who read *What Is Life?* upon its publication.[54]

We come now to what is widely regarded as the most important innovation of the molecular revolution in biology: the enthusiastic, wholesale adoption of the notion of *information*. Information language entered the

---

[54] Consider the following remark by Wilkins: "Schrödinger's book had a very positive effect on me and got me, for the first time, interested in biological problems. I think it had the same effect on other physicists. *I think one reason for this is that Schrödinger wrote as a physicist.* If he had written as an informed macromolecular chemist it probably would not have had the same effect. *The aperiodic crystal idea*, although not so near the truth as the macromolecular idea, *was something which appealed to physicists*" (quoted in Olby 1974: 247, my emphasis). Similarly, Benzer (2002: 15) has noted that "Schrödinger talked about his model of a gene as an aperiodic crystal. And I was struck [...] by the possibility of similarities between solid-state physics and the crystal and gene structure and energy levels of electrons".

biological discourse in the post-war period not once but twice (cf. Keller 1995; Sarkar 1996; Kay 2000), and Schrödinger's influence is evident in both importations, as I will show in a moment. My main contention here is that Schrödinger's explicit principle of order-from-order evolved into a tacit principle of *organization-from-information* that decidedly shaped the agenda of molecular biology. To see how this happened, let us consider the two introductions of information-talk into biology in turn.

The origin of information theory is usually traced to the mathematical theory of communication developed by Claude Shannon in a 1948 paper, which was republished in book form the following year with an introductory essay by Warren Weaver (Shannon and Weaver 1949).[55] Shannon was concerned with the engineering problem of increasing the accuracy of the transmission of a message between sender and receiver. His concept of information is a measure of the uncertainty involved in this communication process; its numerical value is determined by a probabilistic function that formally resembles Boltzmann's entropy formula in thermodynamics. This prompted Shannon (on the advice of von Neumann) to repurpose the term 'entropy' for use in this new context.[56]

The year 1948 also saw the publication of Norbert Wiener's *Cybernetics: Control and Communication in the Animal and the Machine*, which despite its mathematical content became an international bestseller and helped make the new transdisciplinary field of cybernetics a worldwide cultural phenomenon in the 1950s. Wiener's formal treatment of information, like Shannon's, also made use of the concept of entropy, but he defined the former as the negative of the latter, citing Schrödinger's proposal of 'negative entropy' in *What Is Life?* when making this identification (Wiener 1948: 18–19). Shortly thereafter, Léon Brioullin (1949, 1956) developed Wiener's notion and rebranded it as 'negentropy'—also crediting Schrödinger with the original insight.

---

[55] Weaver, as is well known, made key contributions of his own to molecular biology. For one thing, he coined the term 'molecular biology' in 1938. But more importantly still, as director of the natural sciences division of the Rockefeller Foundation between 1932 and 1954, he was responsible for funding much of the research that led to the rise of molecular biology (see Kay 1993). What has *not* been generally recognized, however, is that also in 1948 Weaver published an influential paper titled 'Science and Complexity' (1948) where he implicitly drew on Schrödinger's distinction between order-from-disorder (which he called 'disorganized complexity') and order-from-order (which he called 'organized complexity') to argue that scientific progress during the following fifty years would be dependent on our ability to solve problems of the latter type.

[56] The oft-told story is that von Neumann told Shannon to call his uncertainty measure 'entropy' because "no one knows what entropy really is, so in a debate you will always have the advantage" (quoted in Tribus and McIrvine 1971: 180).

The attempt to apply information theory to biology was an unmitigated failure. It is probably best exemplified by the Quixotic efforts of Henry Quastler, who employed Shannon's formalisms in the hope of transforming biology into an information science (see Kay 2000: 115–127). The proceedings of a symposium he organized in 1952, titled *Essays on the Use of Information Theory in Biology* (Quastler 1953), are replete with astonishing calculations of the 'information content' of various biological entities, from genes and proteins to cells and organisms. A human being, according to one estimate, was deemed to contain 5×10^{25} bits of information!

Wiener, for his part, corresponded with Haldane, who conveyed his enthusiasm about the mathematical arguments in *Cybernetics*—though that was probably because he was one of the very few biologists who could actually understand them. One of Haldane's collaborators at University College London, Hans Kalmus, did publish a paper on the potential of Wiener's framework for genetics (i.e., Kalmus 1950), but it was completely ignored and promptly forgotten, being cited only once by another author until historians rediscovered it in the 1990s. Finally, Brillouin's theoretical notion of negentropy was only seriously taken up by a few biologists, most notably by his compatriot Lwoff, who devoted considerable attention to it—as well as to Schrödinger's idea of negative entropy—in his 1960 Compton Lectures at MIT, later published as *Biological Order* (Lwoff 1962, see especially chapter 6).[57]

On the whole, these technical accounts of information proved too abstruse and too unwieldly to be of any real use in biological research. An important limitation is their exclusive focus on the syntactic aspects of a message; they say nothing about its semantic content (i.e., its *meaning*), which is what biologists are most likely to care about. Shannon himself was well aware of this, and he often cautioned others against the improper application of information theory outside the realms of communication and engineering (see, e.g., Shannon 1956). Wiener, by contrast, promoted the idea of information as part of his cybernetic worldview with almost messianic zeal. Information, for Wiener, was not just a new measure,

---

[57] Schrödinger himself does not appear to have been convinced by Brillouin's information-theoretical account of negative entropy. In a 1953 letter to Brioullin, Schrödinger wrote: "I fully acknowledge the interesting *analogy* between information and 'negentropy', but I considered it inadequate to identify the two. [...] It is difficult to assess the negentropy represented by the *organization* of a steam-engine or a cat or an oak-tree, or the body of Max Born. But I believe that in all these cases there is a great discrepancy between the insignificant thermodynamic value of the negentropy and the significance these organizations have for us" (quoted in Kay 2000: 65).

but a new kind of basic ingredient of the universe, existing in its own distinct domain. "Information is information," he proclaimed, "not matter or energy. No materialism which does not admit this can survive at the present day" (Wiener 1948: 155). His collaborations with physiologists such as Arturo Rosenblueth and Walter Cannon also meant that Wiener, unlike Shannon, not only recognized, but went out of his way to stress the underlying similarities between organisms and servomechanisms, effectively eliminating any ontological barriers still separating the biological from the mechanical (recall that the subtitle of *Cybernetics* is *Control and Communication in the Animal and the Machine*). In tirelessly promoting his cybernetic cause, Wiener targeted the biologists even more so than the physicists—he spoke not of order (as Schrödinger had done) but of *organization*, which is the all-important biological keyword that he strategically chose to identify with information.

When the concept of information finally infiltrated the biological discourse, it did so alongside a whole battery of related (and, at the time, fashionable) cybernetic terms—for example, 'code', 'message', 'feedback', 'control', 'program'—that were applied loosely and metaphorically. It is in this non-technical, non-mathematical sense that 'information' re-entered biology in 1953 when Watson and Crick famously suggested in their second *Nature* paper on the double helix model of DNA that "the precise sequence of the bases is the code which carries the genetical information" (Watson and Crick 1953b: 965). Information *theory* might have been a biological dead end, but information *language* quickly proved to be tremendously productive in guiding experimental research into the structure and function of cellular macromolecules. Perhaps most significantly, information-talk helped make intelligible the vital connection between nucleic acids and proteins (see, e.g., Gamow 1955). As Crick memorably argued—echoing Wiener—in his seminal 1958 paper 'On Protein Synthesis', the crucial relation between DNA, RNA, and protein is not the flow of matter, or the flow energy, but the *flow of information*, clarifying that "[i]nformation means here the *precise* determination of sequence, either of bases in the nucleic acid or of amino acid residues in the protein" (Crick 1958: 153).

Moreover, in adding the proviso that information always flows from nucleic acid to protein but never the reverse—a contention he lightheartedly dubbed the 'Central Dogma' due to the absence of the required evidence to confirm it—Crick established the genocentric, order-from-order logic of molecular biology that Schrödinger had envisaged. The genetic material has a privileged causal (and therefore explanatory) role because it stores, replicates, and transmits the hereditary information. It also *directs* and *controls* the synthesis of proteins and is thus indirectly responsible for all cellular operations. The Central Dogma came to be described in textbooks with the catchy slogan that every student of molecular biology learns: '*DNA makes RNA makes protein*'.

There is something unmistakably Schrödingerian about the conflation in this slogan of the *specification* of a message with the *command* to carry it out; it is hard not to be reminded of Schrödinger's description of the hereditary code-script. Keller has also noticed this: "If the genetic code is a message", she writes, "it is a very particular kind of message: it is an order. Cast in the imperative, it says, 'Make an enzyme!' As Schrödinger so aptly observed, this is no ordinary code: it is 'law-code and executive power in one'" (Keller 1995: 95). The conflation nevertheless proved to be extremely fertile, leading eventually, as I argued in Section 3, to Jacob and Monod's formulation of the genetic program in 1961, with its exaltation of DNA as the 'master molecule' in charge of the cell and of development—just as Schrödinger's code-script is.

I now wish to argue further that molecular biology's understanding of cellular order assumes two distinct kinds of specificity—informational (or genetic) and structural (or spatial)—that represent elaborations (in the case of the first) and vindications (in the case of the second) of ideas we already find in *What Is Life?*.

Informational specificity can be inferred directly from Crick's (1958: 153) definition of information quoted earlier. It is the postulate that the semantic content of a genetic message is specified by the exact arrangement ("*precise* determination") of the linear order ("sequence") in which its elements ("bases" or "amino acid residues") follow each other in aperiodic succession. As we saw in Section 2, Schrödinger tacitly relied on this very same postulate to justify the existence of his code-script. A non-repetitive yet "well-ordered association of atoms", he reasoned, "appears to be the only conceivable material structure that offers a variety of possible ('isomeric') arrangements, sufficiently large to embody a complicated system of 'determinations'" that could "precisely correspond with a highly [...] specified plan of development" (Schrödinger 1944: 61–62). Although Schrödinger did not suggest that the code-script needs to be deciphered (in the way that it was later found that the information encoded in the DNA must be 'transcribed' and 'translated'), he did clearly indicate that its semantic content (the "plan of development") is determined by what molecular biologists after Crick 1958 came to understand as the postulate of informational specificity.

Structural specificity is an equally important postulate in molecular biology. The flow of information from nucleic acid to protein described by the Central Dogma only takes us from nucleotide sequence to the corresponding amino acid sequence—this is what Crick referred to as the 'Sequence Hypothesis' in his influential 1958 paper. However, most cellular functions are performed by proteins folded in space, which often interact and associate with other proteins to form complexes and networks. This is where structural specificity comes in. It is based on the old chemical principle of 'stereospecificity', or 'stereocomplementarity', which dates all the way back to Emil Fischer's lock-and-key model of the enzyme–substrate relation of 1894. It was later extended to immunology by Paul Ehrlich to understand the antibody–antigen relation. But it was Pauling who developed a general theory of stereocomplementarity in the 1940s that he argued applied to all biological processes at the molecular level, and which became foundational for molecular biology (Mertens 2019). It was used by Watson and Crick to understand the complementary relation between nucleotide bases in the DNA double helix, and more broadly to explain the process of molecular recognition that underlies the functions of most proteins, as well as the way proteins come together to form larger assemblies in the cell. What proteins do when they interact with other molecules (including other proteins) is determined by the uniqueness of their shape, or 'conformation', which is itself determined by the precise sequence of their amino acid 'building blocks'. This led to a general theoretical picture of how the virtual, one-dimensional order encoded in the genes (*information*) results in the material, four-dimensional order manifested by the cell (*organization*). Schrödinger's order-from-order thus became molecular biology's organization-from-information.

Although the postulate of structural specificity developed completely independently of *What Is Life?*, there is an important sense in which Schrödinger's argument helped consolidate it as a fundamental pillar of molecular biology (cf. Kupiec 2009, 2010). It relates to the emphasis that stereocomplementarity places on *stability* and *rigidity* as necessary attributes of macromolecules. The timely execution of cellular operations relies on the ability of proteins to discriminate each other's conformations and physically interlock by means of non-covalent linkage sites to form transient stereospecific complexes. In turn, this requires them to adopt perfectly complementary geometric shapes that fit exactly into one another, so as to exclude all other potential binding partners. It is therefore necessary for their structure to be rigid and stable—like a *solid*—as only then can they achieve the extreme specificity that is required for their function.[58]

This is precisely the view of macromolecular interactions that, as I indicated earlier, follows directly from the argument in *What Is Life?*. Although Schrödinger appeals to physical rather than to chemical considerations, the conclusion he arrives at is essentially the same: the functionally important components of the cell (i.e., the nucleic acids and proteins) *must* be stable, rigid structures that behave like solids, or *crystals*, which interact with one another *specifically* and *deterministically* (rather than generically and statistically) like cogs in a microscopic machine, thereby escaping the stochastic perturbations that are typical of the molecular realm.

This mechanical, deterministic, and genocentric conception of life that became dominant with the rise of molecular biology—and which was ardently promoted in popular books such as *Biological Order* (Lwoff 1962), *Of Molecules and Men* (Crick 1966), *Chance and Necessity* (Monod 1972), and *The Logic of Life* (Jacob 1973)—was not strictly speaking new. It has a distinctively Cartesian flavour, as many commentators have observed.[59] Nevertheless, it constituted a radical departure from the biological views that had prevailed in the immediately preceding decades. Earlier biochemical and physiological research (e.g., Needham 1936; Schoenheimer 1942; see also Nicholson 2018) had tended to emphasize the plastic and dynamic character of biological systems, reflected in the continuous metabolic turnover of their material constitution, as well as in the highly heterogeneous nature of their underlying processes, assumed to be subject to stochasticity and only statistically predictable.

Although I certainly would not want to claim that Schrödinger is fully, or even primarily, responsible for prompting this ontological shift in mid-twentieth-century biology—the story, as with everything in history, is obviously more messy and complicated—I do want to suggest that *What Is Life?* played a hitherto unappreciated role in shaping and consolidating molecular biology's theoretical understanding of cellular order. As this section has shown, there was no twenty-year lag between the book's publication and its reception (as some historians would have us believe), even if the book did acquire a new political significance in the mid 1960s when

---

[58] This is appropriately reflected in the etymology of the word 'stereospecificity', which literally means 'solid specificity'.

[59] This, of course, is also true of *What Is Life?*. As Michel Morange (2020: 411) succinctly puts it, "Schrödinger's position is a direct transposition of the mechanistic and deterministic views of Descartes, expressed in terms of genes and chromosomes".

it began to be used as a propagandistic tool to boost the epistemic prestige of molecular biology. I actually agree with Kay when she writes that "Schrödinger's four-dimensional Raphaelesque pattern [contained in the code-script] was digitalized and collapsed into a one-dimensional Boolean message inscribed on a magnetic tape" (Kay 2000: 66). Where I disagree with her is that I take this reformulation of Schrödinger's ideas in the language of information and cybernetics to be evidence of their *continued influence*, not of their initial neglect and subsequent 'reinvention'.

While I have made the case for Schrödinger's impact on molecular biology in general terms, one could also make it by attending to the intellectual trajectories of individual scientists (so that we do not have to rely only on their retrospective autobiographical declarations). In a recent study, Laurent Loison has done just that in relation to Monod, showing that his biological thinking was profoundly affected by his reading of *What Is Life?* (Loison 2015). Monod's case is particularly interesting because, unlike other pioneers of molecular biology who originally came from physics, he was trained as a biologist from the outset. This means that he was taught to think about life in terms of the very principles he would later repudiate as a champion of molecular biology. Though initially concerned with providing statistical, non-deterministic explanations of biological regularities (such as the exponential growth of bacterial cultures), Monod later came to adopt the exact opposite conception, interpreting cellular order as a product of the rigid, clockwork-like precision of its macromolecular components. And one of the key factors that led him to change his mind was Schrödinger's argument in *What Is Life?*.

Evidence for this can be found in Monod's unpublished manuscripts and lecture notes. For example, in the notes for his 1958 Dunham Lectures at Harvard, Monod directly credits Schrödinger for having emphasized the very features—*stability* and *rigidity*—that came to characterize molecular biology's understanding of macromolecules (Figure 8). Elsewhere in his notes, Monod comments on the "very high precision" of "the protein-synthesizing process", and again mentions Schrödinger when observing that the ribosome "appears to work mechanically, like a clock or a precision machine tool, rather than statistically (like what?) (Schrödinger)" (quoted in Loison 2015: 396).

This crucial distinction between *mechanical* and *statistical* forms of order, which lies at the core of Schrödinger's argument in *What Is Life?*, is one that Monod repeatedly invokes to illustrate the difference between the 'old' and the 'new' biology. Consider the following remark from *Enzymatic Cybernetics*, a book-length French-language manuscript

> proteins. The whole trend of modern molecular biology makes it every day clearer that structural stability and rigidity rather than dynamicity are the most essential and characteristic properties of the typical cellular macromolecules.

> SCHRODINGER, with the insight of genius, had perceived this as a necessary attribute of heredity material. The validity of this view is now beautifully demonstrated, for DNA, by the work of LEVINTHAL and others. But stability and rigidity are apparently not limited to DNA. Recent work shows conclusively that the bulk of cellular high-molecular RNA is stable and non-dynamic in healthy, growing cells and the same, as we have just seen, is true of protein. The "dynamic state

Figure 8 Excerpt from Monod's unpublished lecture notes for his 1958 Dunham Lectures at Harvard in which Schrödinger is mentioned
(reproduced with permission of the Pasteur Institute Archives)

completed in 1960 that Monod never got round to publishing in his lifetime (it was finally published in 2021):

> The natural tendency of experimenters who have studied elementary cellular processes has been to interpret these phenomena in terms of the fundamental laws of classical physics and chemistry, which are statistical laws and are all ultimately reducible to the gas laws. But with each passing day it is becoming increasingly clear that the elementary phenomena of cellular physiology are not reducible to statistical laws, but rather to mechanisms revealing a precise construction and complex circuits like those of a machine. (Monod 2021 [1960]: 59; my translation)[60]

Furthermore, Monod makes it clear that Schrödinger's ideas were absolutely critical to this transition. This is how he dramatically expresses the point in a public lecture delivered in Geneva in 1965:

> Theoretically liberated, by Schrödinger's perspectives, from the paradox that made biology a science the object of which seemed to escape the absolutely general law of entropy, modern biology has been effectively able to describe—in principle if not in detail—the essential properties of living beings in terms of *molecular structures*. (Monod 1966: 43–44; my translation)

---

[60] Monod makes very similar assertions when explaining to Judson what sets molecular biology apart from the older physicochemical approaches to biology of the early twentieth century (see Judson 1979: 210–211).

Monod's philosophy of molecular biology was presented in mature form in his widely read *Chance and Necessity* (1972), whose revealing subtitle is *An Essay on the Natural Philosophy of Modern Biology*. In many ways, this book represents the fully fledged realization of Schrödinger's biological vision, even though *What Is Life?* is not actually cited, presumably because by then its message had been fully assimilated and had become too familiar to require mentioning.

Loison (2015) has interestingly suggested that we can think of Monod's theoretical agenda in molecular biology between 1950 and 1970 as an attempt to identify the new order-from-order laws or principles that Schrödinger expected would be eventually discovered. These would ostensibly include many of the tenets we have discussed in this section, such as informational and structural specificity, Crick's Central Dogma, and his and Jacob's concept of the genetic program. If this is the right way to think about this history, then Schrödinger's order-from-order research program can only be regarded a resounding success.

Be that as it may, the subsequent development of molecular biology in the late twentieth century only served to further consolidate Schrödinger's mechanical, deterministic, and genocentric view of the cell. Monod (1972: 98) had already claimed that "[w]ith the globular protein we already have, at the molecular level, a veritable machine". Thereafter, the 'molecular machine' concept came to be used to characterize most functionally specialized macromolecular complexes in the cell (Alberts 1998; Frank 2011; see also Nicholson 2019). Similarly, the postulate of structural specificity was invoked to justify the appeal to wiring diagrams and design charts in schematic representations of metabolic, regulatory, and signalling pathways, which are still today frequently depicted as fixed, solid-state circuits deliberately made to resemble the circuit boards of electronic engineering. A typical example is reproduced in Figure 9.

Now, as I anticipated at the end of Section 1, one of the reasons why it really does matter that Schrödinger is (at least partly) responsible for molecular biology's view of the cell is that much of this view is increasingly at odds with experimental findings. Since the turn of the twenty-first century, a growing number of biologists have been systematically calling into question many of its ontological assumptions (see, e.g., Rose 1998; Kirschner et al. 2000; Lewontin 2000; Oyama et al. 2001; Moss 2003; Woese 2004; Karsenti 2008; Kupiec 2010; Heams 2014; Noble 2016; Ball 2023).

We already discussed in Section 3 some of the major problems with the genetic program, and with genocentric, order-from-order explanations of cellular activities more generally. And in Section 4 we saw how statistical (as

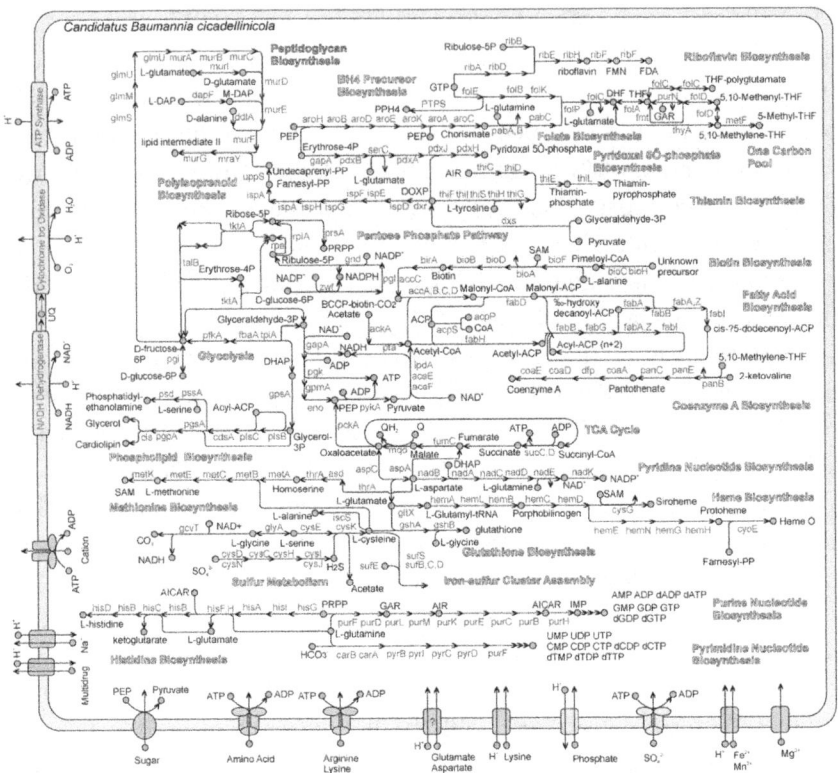

Figure 9 Wiring diagram of metabolic pathways in the bacterium *Baumannia cicadellinicola* depicted as a solid-state circuit board (adapted from Wu et al. 2006)

opposed to mechanical) models are increasingly being used to understand the molecular basis of development, as well as how non-classical instances of order-from-disorder not foreseen by Schrödinger (such as reaction–diffusion systems and other self-organizing processes) are now acknowledged to play an indispensable role in the generation and maintenance of order at the cellular and multicellular levels. In much the same way, recent research has shown many of the ideas we have discussed in this section to be seriously problematic. However, as I have already examined these problems at length in previous work (i.e., Nicholson 2019, 2020), I shall resist the temptation of doing so again here. Instead, let me just mention some of the most pertinent and surprising findings, and the interested reader can consult the aforementioned publications for the full analysis.

Stability and rigidity, it turns out, are not necessary features of biological macromolecules. The structure of proteins in their native state is *soft* and *fluid*, not hard and rigid. Far from displaying a single conformation, most proteins stochastically alternate between different ordered states. Many proteins (known as 'intrinsically disordered proteins') do not have an ordered conformation *at all* but instead roam the cell as unfolded polypeptide chains capable of binding to a wide range of substrates. *Promiscuity*, not specificity, is the rule for most proteins (including enzymes): what a protein does in the cell is as much a product of its *cellular context* as its amino acid sequence. The same polypeptide chain can partake in a variety of functions depending on when and where it is expressed, and on what partners it associates with (a phenomenon sometimes referred to as 'moonlighting').

Protein-protein interactions are not stereospecific interlockings but probabilistic collision events—they are *contingent* and *opportunistic*, not the solid-state manifestation of a pre-existing genetic blueprint. This is why circuit-like depictions like Figure 9 can be so misleading. There is no wiring physically connecting the proteins as there is in a real electronic circuit; the 'wiring' in such diagrams rather reflects the questionable reification of ethereal 'information flows'. Moreover, the depicted network of proteins represents only *one* of the potentially innumerable ways in which those same proteins might interact at different times and under different conditions. Larger macromolecular assemblies (e.g., ribosomes) also lack the structural rigidity and operational precision of what might be expected of true 'molecular machines', and they move *stochastically* rather than mechanically when performing their functions.[61]

Overall, there is something decidedly odd about the habit of molecular biologists to downplay stochasticity, if not to disregard it altogether, in their representations and explanations. After all, stochasticity is a well-understood physical phenomenon known as far back as the nineteenth century to be inescapable at the molecular scale at any temperature above absolute zero. If I may be allowed to end this section on a more speculative note, perhaps this is, in the final analysis, the real legacy of *What Is Life?*. It is not inconceivable that Schrödinger's theoretical view of the cell as a microscopic clockwork operating deterministically according to non-statistical, mechanical principles granted molecular biologists the license to dismiss the effects of stochasticity (despite being inevitable from a strictly physical point of view), freeing them up to focus on meticulously characterizing

---

[61] As a prominent ribosome researcher puts it, "all the functionally significant movements of the ribosome [...] are biased random walks, and it is most unlikely that any given ribosome will ever do exactly the same thing twice as it elongates some polypeptide" (Moore 2012: 8). Notice how this directly contradicts Monod's Schrödingerian characterization of the ribosome in 1958 as "a clock or a precision machine tool" (quoted in Loison 2015: 396).

the structure of individual macromolecules—drawing attention to their crystal-like rigidity (ostensibly confirmed by the use of available methods like X-ray crystallography) and emphasizing their functional specificity (assumed to be genetically determined)—all while largely ignoring the turbulent, destabilizing influences of their physical milieu. One can easily imagine how this attitude might have encouraged the appeal to conceptual models borrowed from the macroscopic domain—where stochastic fluctuations *are* negligible and *can* be safely ignored—such as the highly suggestive engineering metaphors spawned by cybernetics and, later, computer science that, as we have seen, are so distinctive of molecular biology.

6 Understanding Schrödinger's Motives in *What Is Life*?

In the preceding sections, we have taken Schrödinger to task for having promoted an inappropriately genocentric view of living systems, which he assumed to operate deterministically in a way that wrongly ignored the effects of stochasticity on their underlying molecular processes. Now, the reader might feel a bit uneasy about indictments issued with the benefit of hindsight, as it would be unfair to chastise Schrödinger for making claims whose problems only became apparent many years (or even decades) later. This would be as absurd as blaming him for failing to predict the future course of science. One can certainly think of criticisms of *What Is Life?* that would be unjust for this reason—for instance, if we scolded Schrödinger for believing that the hereditary substance is protein rather than DNA, or for not having recognized that self-organizing processes are a crucial form of order-from-disorder in living systems.

One of my aims in this section is to demonstrate that the criticisms I have presented of Schrödinger's conception of cellular order do not fall under this category. The reason is that there is nothing necessary or inevitable about this conception—either today *or in 1944*. Schrödinger's biological views, far from mirroring the conventional wisdom of the historical period when they were formulated, were not even orthodox in their own time. Instead, they reflect *deliberate choices* that Schrödinger made when he was working out the argument that he would later present in *What Is Life?*. To see why Schrödinger chose to argue the way he did in his book, we first need to identify his motives for turning to biological issues in the first place.

This is not a trivial question. Why would a 56-year-old theoretical physicist with no formal training in biology decide to take on the thorny subject of 'the physical aspect of the living cell' and go on to publish an entire book about it? A number of hypotheses have been proposed to explain this. Some have suggested that Schrödinger's interest in biology can be traced back to his childhood. His father, Rudolf Schrödinger, had a lifelong amateur interest in botany—he wrote several papers on the phylogeny of plants, and at the time of his death he was vice-president of the Zoological–Botanical Society of Vienna (Moore 1989: 116)—so it is possible that conversations at home instilled in him a love for biology at an early age.[62] In his *Autobiographical Sketches*, written at the end of his life, Schrödinger recalled how as a schoolboy he "virtually devoured *The Origin of Species*" and "soon became an ardent follower of Darwinism" (Schrödinger 1992: 174–175).

Later, as a student at the University of Vienna, Schrödinger became fascinated by Richard Semon's book *The Mneme as a Conservative Principle* (1904)—a highly speculative Lamarckian treatise that sought to explain the phenomena of heredity, development, instinct, and consciousness using the concept of a 'mneme', a sort of cellular repository of organismic memory that Semon claimed governed all biological processes. According to Schrödinger's biographer Walter Moore, Semon's book "had a major influence on the development of his philosophical ideas" (Moore 1989: 46). In 1925, just before his monumental discovery of wave mechanics, he wrote a long essay expounding his philosophical views—published decades later as *My View of the World* (Schrödinger 1964)—where he revisited the themes of Semon's book, and which reveals his continued interest in the intriguing idea of a genetic 'memory' preserved through the generations and immune to the ravages of time. Keller (1995), Kay (2000), and Morange (2020) have all argued that this longstanding preoccupation is what drove Schrödinger to write *What Is Life?*.

Others have sought the book's origins in Schrödinger's general intellectual disposition. Neville Symonds (1986), who studied with him in Dublin in the late 1940s, points out that Schrödinger had exceptionally wide interests. He was a modern-day 'renaissance man' with a desire for unified knowledge and who enjoyed making brief intellectual excursions into areas other than his own. Indeed, we should not forget that, besides biology, Schrödinger published booklets (also based on public lectures) on philosophy of science (Schrödinger 1951), the Ancient Greeks (Schrödinger 1954), and the mind-body problem (Schrödinger 1958). A version of this hypothesis was previously advanced by Olby (1971) and it has been put forward again more recently by Gould (1995).

---

[62] Perhaps this is why Schrödinger dedicated *What Is Life?* to the memory of his parents.

While acknowledging that all of the above factors might well have played a role, I suspect that the primary cause for the genesis of the book lies elsewhere. Specifically, what I want to suggest—and here I follow Edward Yoxen (1977, 1979) and Phillip Sloan (2012)—is that it is impossible to make sense of Schrödinger's engagement with biology without carefully considering his position in the heated debates that took place during the interwar period regarding the interpretation and extension of quantum mechanics. As I will show in what follows, only by attending to this context can we understand what Schrödinger is really up to in *What Is Life?*.

The key point to bear in mind when placing Schrödinger in relation to the physics community of his time is that he was fundamentally at odds with most of his contemporaries (with the notable exception of Einstein) regarding the way to interpret the formalizations of quantum mechanics—a science that Schrödinger himself had helped create with his wave mechanics in 1926. While his own wave equation is deterministic, the orthodox interpretation of quantum mechanics articulated by Bohr and Werner Heisenberg, known as the *Copenhagen interpretation*, is not. Schrödinger (like Einstein) could never bring himself to accept this interpretation, and he grew ever more frustrated with its proponents, who invariably reinterpreted his wave mechanics in probabilistic and instrumentalist (i.e., antirealist) terms, much to his dismay.[63]

Feeling increasingly out of step with the dominant paradigm, Schrödinger published a three-part paper in the German-language journal *Die Naturwissenschaften* sardonically titled 'The Present Situation in Quantum Mechanics' (Schrödinger 1935a) where he devised his famous cat thought experiment, which he intended as a *reductio ad absurdum* of the Copenhagen interpretation. Schrödinger imagined a cat inside a sealed box along with a minuscule amount of radioactive material. If this material happens to decay, then a device releases a hammer, which smashes a vial of poison, which kills the cat. If the material does not decay, the cat lives. As radioactive decay is a quantum-mechanical phenomenon, the entire box must be regarded as a giant quantum system. What this means according to the Copenhagen interpretation is that until a measurement

---

[63] During a seminar in Zurich on matrix mechanics—the competing yet mathematically equivalent theory developed by Heisenberg along with Born and Pascual Jordan at the University of Göttingen—Schrödinger is alleged to have angrily complained that "the damned Göttingen people are using my beautiful wave mechanics to compute their shitty little matrix elements" (quoted in Laughlin 2011: 37). Heisenberg, for his part, vented in a letter to Wolfgang Pauli in 1926 that "[t]he more I ponder the physical part of Schrödinger's theory the more abhorrent I find it" adding that "[w]hat Schrödinger writes about the visualizability of his theory […] I find it crap" (ibid.).

is made (i.e., the box is opened and the cat is observed), the cat remains in a blurry indeterminate state of superposition—both dead and alive—which is, of course, absurd. Ironically, though, instead of undermining physicists' confidence in the validity of the Copenhagen interpretation (as Schrödinger had hoped), his cat only served to strengthen it, eventually becoming the definitive symbol of the transcendent weirdness that has come to be generally associated with quantum mechanics.[64]

Schrödinger's distaste for the Copenhagen interpretation has a lot to do with his scientific background, particularly with the enormous influence that Boltzmann exerted on his intellectual development. In his inaugural address to the Prussian Academy of Sciences in 1929, Schrödinger declared that Boltzmann's "line of thought may be called my first love in science. No other has ever thus enraptured me or will ever do so again" (Schrödinger 1935b: 13). Much later, in his *Autobiographical Sketches*, he asserted that "no perception in physics has ever seemed more important to me than that of Boltzmann—despite Planck and Einstein" (Schrödinger 1992: 168).

Besides a lifelong fascination with statistical mechanics (see, e.g., Schrödinger 1946), what Schrödinger inherited from Boltzmann is the philosophical conviction (which Boltzmann propounded in explicit opposition to the phenomenalist attitude urged by Ernst Mach, the other major influence in Vienna at the time) that physical theory should provide realistic, internally consistent, and causally determinate descriptions (or visualizable 'pictures') of the microscopic entities responsible for macroscopic phenomena. This familiar expectation—generally associated with the notion of 'classical physics' (a term that Boltzmann himself coined in 1899)—became progressively eroded in the twentieth century, especially with the rise to prominence of Bohr's views, which encouraged younger physicists to develop mathematical models without worrying about their physical (i.e., spatiotemporal) visualizability. As it became apparent that it would not be possible to provide observer-independent, non-contradictory descriptions of quantum phenomena, Schrödinger became increasingly distraught and alienated from most of his physicist colleagues, who simply accepted the profoundly counterintuitive, observer-dependent, and intrinsically indeterministic character of the Copenhagen interpretation.

For Schrödinger, this attitude towards the atomic world—defined by Bohr's 'principle of complementarity' (which holds that entities can exhibit

---

[64] Schrödinger's cat has become so embedded in the popular imagination that Schrödinger himself is now primarily remembered—among the general public, at least—for the very weirdness of the Copenhagen interpretation that he desperately (yet ultimately unsuccessfully) tried to overcome.

mutually exclusive properties that cannot be measured simultaneously), as well as ideas of 'acausality' and spatiotemporally discontinuous 'jumps'—was bad enough as a theoretical perspective in physics.[65] But what incensed him infinitely more was the *philosophical* use of the Copenhagen interpretation in tackling fundamental problems in domains *beyond* physics; something that Bohr and Jordan both did repeatedly, in different ways, in the contexts of biology and psychology.

In a number of public lectures and papers (collected in Bohr 1999), Bohr suggested that in these two sciences one encounters an epistemological situation that is *analogous* to the one found in atomic physics. Just as light, under different experimental setups, can be described either in terms of waves or of particles but not both simultaneously, life can be described either mechanistically (by means of physicochemical analysis) or teleologically (by means of direct observation) but not both simultaneously—as the former involves killing the organism, thereby destroying its purposive character. The two descriptions stand in a complementary relation, according to Bohr, as they are mutually exclusive yet jointly necessary. Complementarity also obtains in the psychological consideration of mental states, as it is not possible to observe our own thoughts without affecting them in the process. We can either analyze our emotions or experience them, but not both simultaneously. Bohr argued that the age-old dispute between determinism and free will could be solved by viewing it from the perspective afforded by his principle of complementarity.

In a way, Jordan went even further than Bohr. Not content with merely drawing analogies, Jordan argued that quantum mechanics (in its orthodox Copenhagen interpretation) was itself *responsible* for biological and psychological phenomena. In a speculative paper published in *Die Naturwissenschaften* titled 'Quantum Mechanics and the Foundational Problems of Biology and Psychology' (Jordan 1932), and in many other publications thereafter, Jordan articulated his 'amplifier theory' of the organism, which postulates that the acausal behaviour of individual atoms can be amplified through the structure of organic molecules and larger subsystems so as to 'direct' or 'steer' their macroscopic behaviour, thereby transferring acausality to whole organisms. According to Jordan, this amplified acausality of organisms—not explainable in classical or

---

[65] When Schrödinger visited Bohr in Copenhagen in 1926, the two spent several days and nights intensely discussing the meaning of quantum mechanics. Heisenberg later recounted how Schrödinger at one point indignantly told Bohr that "[i]f we are still going to have to put up with these damn quantum jumps, I am sorry that I ever had anything to do with quantum theory" (quoted in Moore 1989: 228).

mechanical terms—is ultimately responsible for our inner experience of free will, which is a manifestation of quantum acausality magnified from the atomic level to neurological processes in the brain.[66]

It is these ideas that I believe provide the right context to understand Schrödinger's incursion into biology, and where we should locate the inception of the argument that would eventually appear in *What Is Life?*. My contention, which I anticipated at the end of Section 1, is that Schrödinger turned to biology because he hoped that he would find in the molecular structure of living matter the means to salvage the mechanical and deterministic worldview of classical physics that he felt had become undermined by the Copenhagen interpretation of quantum mechanics. His chief motivation was to *prevent* proponents of this interpretation from using *biological* phenomena as a stepping stone to ground the claim that *quantum indeterminacy provides a physical foundation for free will* (which Schrödinger thought could not be justified scientifically). He did this by defending the idea that life is at its core a strictly deterministic phenomenon, and that it is deterministic owing to the prodigious stability of its genetic material, which is safeguarded by the Heitler–London theory derived from quantum mechanics. So, quantum mechanics comes to the rescue for Schrödinger, just as it does for Jordan, but what it offers him is the exact opposite: not indeterminacy and freedom, but *determinacy* and *clockwork precision*.[67] By strategically severing the biological link connecting the physical to the neurological (or psychological), free will would need to be accounted for by other, preferably non-scientific, means.

When we look more closely at the circumstances in which Schrödinger developed the argument for *What Is Life?*, we find in them compelling evidence in support of this hypothesis. Let me mention three specific examples (each, incidentally, obtained from a different archival source).

In February 1933, exactly ten years before his 'What Is Life?' lectures in Dublin, Schrödinger gave a talk at the Prussian Academy of Sciences in Berlin titled 'Why Are Atoms So Small?' where he outlined what he later called in *What Is Life?* "the naïve physicist's approach to the subject" (Schrödinger 1944: 4). Indeed, the book includes in its opening chapter a subsection with the same title as his Berlin talk from a decade earlier (i.e., ibid.: 4–6). Interestingly, this talk appears to have been partly conceived in response

---

[66] For a comprehensive examination of Jordan's research program in 'quantum biology', see Beyler 1994. More concise overviews can be found in Wise 1994 and Beyler 1996.

[67] This stark contrast between Schrödinger and Jordan is all the more extraordinary considering the fact that Jordan actually shared Schrödinger's view of the gene as a sort of 'master molecule'.

to the 1932 paper by Jordan that we discussed above. In September 1932, Schrödinger had written to his former colleague Karl Przibram at the Vienna Institute for Radium Research (and brother of Hans Przibram, director of the Vienna Institute for Experimental Biology) about the effects of Brownian motion on microorganisms. When Jordan's paper came out in November, he wrote a second letter in which he referred to it critically. Although Schrödinger's letters to Przibram appear to have been lost, Przibram's second reply—writing also on behalf of his brother Hans—is very revealing:

> We both read Jordan's paper and were also very concerned, my brother was downright outraged. The trick with free will is just too irritating. [...] Do you not consider it appropriate that a reply should appear in *Die Naturwissenschaften*? You would be the man to do it. My brother is at your disposal to advise and collaborate on biological questions. Will your talk appear in print? Perhaps that could offer the opportunity for Jordan's paper to be answered.[68]

Schrödinger never published a reply to Jordan in *Die Naturwissenschaften*; all that appeared in print was a brief summary of his Berlin talk (i.e., Schrödinger 1933). Nevertheless, what survives of his exchange with Przibram indicates a clear connection between Jordan's extravagant attempt to explain free will in terms of amplified quantum indeterminacy in organisms and Schrödinger's desire to tackle questions at the interface of physics and biology—more than a decade before he wrote *What Is Life?*.

A second line of evidence can be found in Schrödinger's correspondence with Donnan in the late 1930s and early 1940s, which provides an insightful, behind-the-scenes look into how the ideas in *What Is Life?* gradually took form. In 1935, Donnan sent Schrödinger an old paper of his (i.e., Donnan 1918) that prefigures one of the central theses of *What Is Life?*, namely that "[t]he essentially 'biological' aspect of the science of living things is that it is fundamentally concerned, not with statistical averages [like physics and chemistry], but with sequences of events pertaining to particular individual units" (ibid.: 285; my translation). In 1943, Donnan sent him another of his papers (i.e., Donnan 1928) that, as I already indicated in Section 4, anticipated Schrödinger's famous discussion in *What Is Life?* of how organisms comply with the second law of thermodynamics. Donnan's 1928 paper also included the remark that "[i]t is difficult to resist the comparison of the developing embryo with the building of a house" and "to the plans of an invisible architect" (ibid.: 1561), which is almost

---

[68] Przibram to Schrödinger, 28 November 1932; my translation. Schrödinger Papers, Austrian Central Library for Physics.

identical to Schrödinger's memorable description of the code-script as "architect's plan and builder's craft—in one" (Schrödinger 1944: 21).[69]

Schrödinger's exchanges with Donnan were partly concerned with the problem of how to account for the autonomy [*Eigengesetzlichkeit*] of living matter in a non-vitalistic way that would not violate the laws of physics and chemistry. The somewhat paradoxical solution that Schrödinger eventually arrived at was to tie the distinctive orderliness of life to the *failure* of statistical physics to adequately explain it. Although statistical physics fails, Schrödinger explains to Donnan that it does so *instructively*, as it allows us

> to understand in a rational and unmystic way the fact that there may be such peculiar arrangements of molecules [in the living cell] to which the ordinary laws of physics do not apply, *not* because there be any mystic interference of *vis viva*, *entelechia* or that kind of nonsense, but because the arrangement of molecules is such, that the *ordinary statistical* methods do not apply, on which the ordinary laws of physics are based.[70]

In privately discussing these matters with Donnan, Schrödinger made telling comments that provide additional support for the hypothesis outlined earlier. For instance, when referring to a paper where Donnan had mathematically described the historical character of organisms with reference to Bohr's principle of complementarity (i.e., Donnan 1936), Schrödinger lamented the "disaster" that "Bohr's sham-philosophy has produced" when applied to other sciences—an application that he irreverently dubbed "Kopenhagen twaddle". He asserted that "physicists do wrong in using their claim of representing the 'fundamental science' to try and impose some petty fundamental methodological principle of *their* science to others".[71] In fact, prompted by Donnan's 1936 paper, Schrödinger published a note in *Nature* titled 'Indeterminism and Free Will' where he criticized the suggestion made by some physicists "that the *apparent indeterminacy* [...] of living matter might be connected with the theoretical indeterminacy of modern physics", adding—revealingly—that their motivation for doing so "is evidently the hope (whether outspoken or concealed) of extracting from the *new* physical dogma a *model of free-will*". Schrödinger argued that this hope is illusory, and that "free-will actions do not call

---

[69] Accordingly, when Schrödinger begins outlining his argument in the opening pages of *What Is Life?*, the only literature that he cites as an influence on his thinking are these "two most inspiring papers by F. G. Donnan" (Schrödinger 1944: 3).
[70] Schrödinger to Donnan, 26 October 1942. Donnan Papers, Special Collections, University College London.
[71] Schrödinger to Donnan, 24 January 1943. Donnan Papers, Special Collections, University College London.

for a special 'indeterminist' explanation any more than other events" (Schrödinger 1936: 13).

Schrödinger's correspondence with Darlington offers further evidence for my hypothesis. When *What Is Life?* was nearing publication, Schrödinger wrote to Darlington to ask permission to use some of his illustrations. Darlington replied, granting Schrödinger the permission he requested, and expressing his delight that a physicist of his calibre had taken up problems in genetics, despite admitting that he often quarrelled with physicists over the 'question of indeterminacy'. Schrödinger's response is enormously revealing, not just because it shows, once again, his underlying concern with free will, but because it lays his cards on the table in a way that clearly discloses what he was trying to do in *What Is Life?*. He begins by assuring Darlington that his quarrel over indeterminacy is not with him, and then writes the following by way of explanation:

> Some physicists, among them [some] of the greatest (Niels Bohr, Sommerfeld, Jordan) have played about with this indeterminacy question in relation to living matter in a way which I consider illegitimate and mischievous (though their *sincerity* is beyond doubt, but in philosophy they are children). Even the old problem (if it is a problem?!) of Free Will is occasionally supposed to have been cleared up by that blessed indeterminacy and by alleged very recent results of physics (!) on the relation between the observer and his object (my mark of exclamation means to say, that I do not think physics alone is competent for that, and also not physics in the first place). At any rate I believe that with regard to living matter the outstanding feature we are called upon to understand and to explain is the incredibly strict *determinacy*. Quantum theory is needed to explain this *determinacy*, as it were to *protect* the hereditary substance against the continual impact of disorderly heat motion (which may be a less fundamental, but is practically a much more important reason for lack of complete determination of [biological] events than Heisenberg's minute uncertainty).[72]

Schrödinger's motives were clear—at least to Darlington. In one of the most perspicacious analyses of *What Is Life?*, Darlington explains that the main takeaway of Schrödinger's book is that the extreme stability of the chromosome molecules "enables the organism [...] to escape to a very large extent the quantum indeterminacy of inorganic matter. *We can no longer skip merrily (as some did a short while ago) from quantum mechanics to free will. The organism now has a say in the matter*" (Darlington and Mather 1950: 170, my emphasis).

---

[72] Schrödinger to Darlington, undated [ca. June 1943]. DIAS Archives.

Only in the light of the above considerations, I think, does it become possible to understand why Schrödinger insisted on adding his quirky epilogue 'On Determinism and Free Will' to *What Is Life?*, despite not having been part of the original lectures, and not being obviously connected to their content. They also explain why, with the proofs already in hand, Schrödinger chose not to go ahead with the book's publication when the initial Irish publisher made it conditional on him removing the epilogue, as we noted back in Section 1.[73] Although to the biological reader the epilogue is *by far* the least relevant, least convincing, and most muddled section of the entire book (and this is as true today as it was in 1944), if the argument presented here is correct, then it is also perhaps the most significant for understanding *why* the book was written. And not because of *what* the epilogue actually claims, but because of Schrödinger's dogged determination to include it as his "own, necessarily subjective" five-page philosophical coda to his 86-page examination of 'the physical aspect of the living cell' (Schrödinger 1944: 87).[74]

Nevertheless, because Schrödinger made no effort to make his intentions clear (neither Jordan nor Bohr are cited or even mentioned in *What Is Life?*), the point of his epilogue was lost on most readers, who found it perplexing, slightly embarrassing, and not worthy of comment—unless, of course, it was to mock it, and neither Haldane (1945) nor Muller (1946) missed the opportunity to do so in their respective reviews of the book, as we noted at the end of Section 2. An interesting exception here is Delbrück, who in his own review of *What Is Life?* quoted Schrödinger's revealing declaration in the epilogue that "contrary to the opinion upheld in some quarters, *quantum indeterminacy* plays no biologically relevant role" in the cell (Schrödinger 1944: 87), and then perceptively inferred that "[t]he opinions here referred to are presumably those of Bohr and those of Jordan" (Delbrück 1945: 371).[75]

---

[73] Notice also that the epilogue's title is featured in a surprisingly prominent manner on the dust jacket of the book's first edition (recall Figure 2b). This conspicuous mention of the epilogue has been omitted in more recent reprintings of *What Is Life?*.

[74] Schrödinger discussed the implications of Vedanta philosophy much more extensively in *My View of the World* (1964). He also considered the bearing of quantum mechanics on free will at the end of *Science and Humanism* (1951), where, after describing and criticizing the positions of Jordan and of Bohr on the matter, he concluded that "quantum physics has nothing to do with the free-will problem. If there is such a problem, it is not furthered a whit by the latest development in physics" (ibid.: 67). This mirrors the remarks he published fifteen years earlier (i.e., Schrödinger 1936: 13) that we quoted above.

[75] That Delbrück would be one of the few readers to pick up on this is not entirely surprising given his own background in theoretical physics and his lifelong fascination with Bohr's ideas of complementarity, which actually inspired him to reorient his career towards

We can now return to the point with which we started, when I suggested that the conception of cellular order that we find in *What Is Life?* is not one that a non-biologist would have reasonably inferred upon becoming acquainted with the pertinent technical literature. It is rather a conception that reflects the particular philosophical agenda that drove Schrödinger to develop an interest in the topic—an agenda that we have uncovered in the preceding pages. One consequence of this is that, in his hope of finding in living matter a way of salvaging the deterministic worldview of classical physics, and in striving to keep it from becoming further eroded by the shocking indeterminacy discovered at the heart of quantum mechanics, Schrödinger only read biological literature that validated his existing deterministic predilections. The uncompromisingly genocentric view of the cell and of development that Schrödinger defended in *What Is Life?* is not one that he could have extracted from the writings of most biochemists and embryologists of the time (should he had taken the time to read them)—it would not even had been the obvious message to derive from the work of most *geneticists* of that period. But it *was* the view best suited for him to make the case he wanted to make.

There is plenty of evidence for this. For example, the Schrödinger Papers at the Austrian Central Library for Physics contain a notebook labelled 'Warum' (Figure 10), which Schrödinger used to prepare his Berlin talk of 1933 ('Warum' is the first word of the talk's original German title: '*Warum sind die Atome so klein?*'). Of particular interest is a small card enclosed within it (also reproduced in Figure 10) where Schrödinger wrote down the papers that he read in preparation, presumably after his correspondence with the Przibram brothers in late 1932. These are: Alexander and Bridges 1929, Boycott 1929, Hetler and Bronfenbrenner 1929, and Muller 1929. Out of the four, Muller's paper is by far the longest and most substantive, and the 'Warum' notebook shows that Schrödinger studied it carefully (see also Sloan 2012 for a complementary analysis of Muller's influence on Schrödinger).

The reason why this matters is that Muller's views on the gene, which we examined back in Section 3, stand—particularly as presented in the 1929 manifesto that Schrödinger studied—as some of the most fervently reductionistic and deterministic expressed by *any* geneticist in the first third, if not the first half, of the twentieth century. They certainly did not reflect the views of most geneticists (let alone most embryologists and biochemists),

---

biology in the 1930s. Bohr's influence on Delbrück has received considerable scholarly attention; see, for example, Kay 1985, Roll-Hansen 2000, McKaughan 2005, Sloan and Fogel 2011, and Sloan 2025.

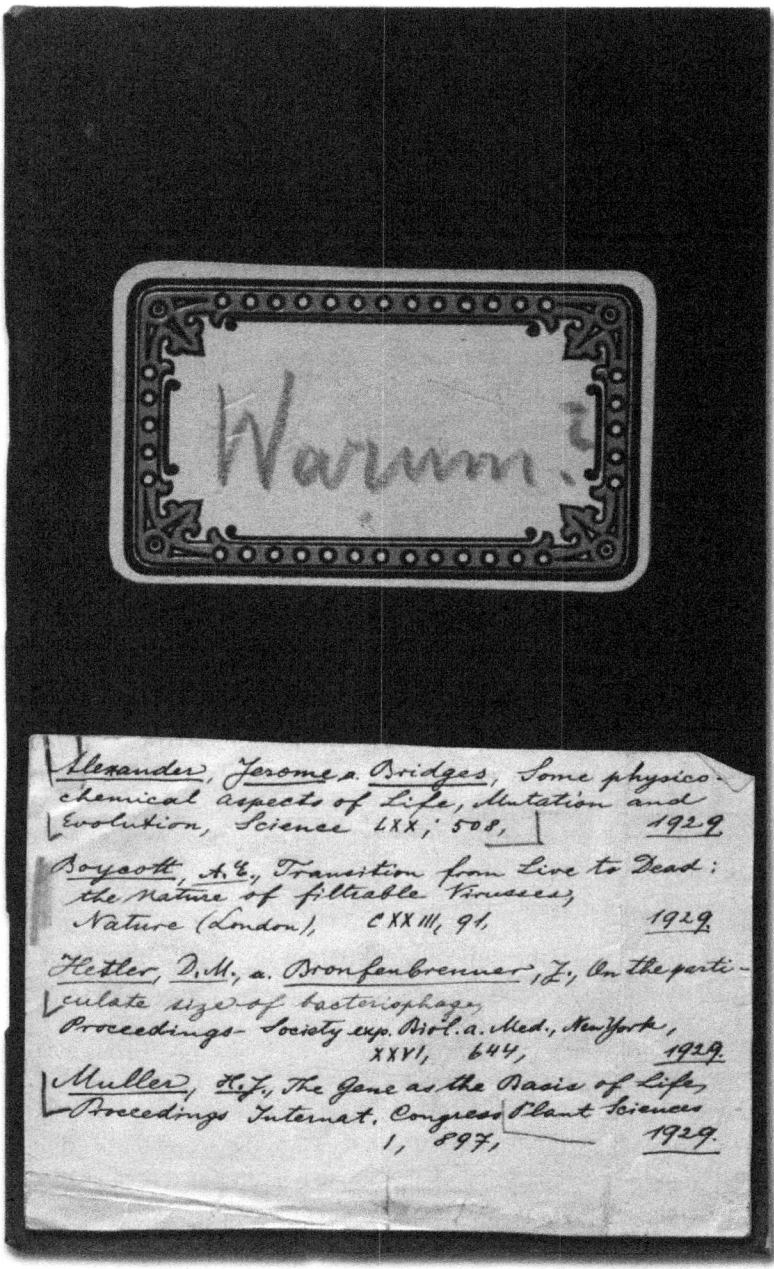

Figure 10 Front cover of the notebook Schrödinger used to prepare his Berlin talk of 1933 with an enclosed card listing some of the biological literature that he read in preparation
(reproduced with permission of the Austrian Central Library for Physics)

at least not at that time. To learn that Schrödinger was so taken with them in the early 1930s, precisely when his biological ideas were starting to take shape, helps explain why, although Muller's work is not even cited in *What Is Life?*, it is really Muller's views—much more than Delbrück's (which *are* discussed at great length)—that Schrödinger channelled in the book when he proposed his genocentric, order-from-order conception of the cell, as I already suggested in Section 3.

This becomes even more apparent when we compare Delbrück's views as presented in TZD (the key claims of which we reviewed in Section 3) with the interpretation that Schrödinger gave of them in *What Is Life?*. As Sloan has acutely observed (Sloan 2012; see also his co-authored introduction to TZD in Sloan and Fogel 2011), Schrödinger *misrepresented* the main conclusions of TZD in order to make them consistent with his own genocentric and deterministic commitments.[76]

The Mullerian view of the gene that Schrödinger defends so enthusiastically in *What Is Life?* is actually described in TZD, specifically in the penultimate paragraph of the paper's closing theoretical summary, which was most likely written by Delbrück:

> Some attempts have been made to project back theoretically, by way of the hereditarily-modifiable, ontogenetic developmental sequences, from the organism to its individual genes. The genes are thus conceived as the immediate 'starting points' of the chains of reactions comprising the developmental processes. [...] [T]he cell, thus far proving itself so magnificently as the unit of life, dissolves into the 'ultimate units of life', the genes. (TZD, quoted in Sloan 2012: 148)

Crucially, however, in the paper's final paragraph, this Mullerian view is emphatically rejected by the authors:

> *Our ideas about the gene challenge this picture.* Genes are [...] likely incapable of directly forming the morphogenic substances; they also can hardly be thought of as the 'starting points' of developmental sequences. [...] Therefore, we need not dissolve the cell into genes, and the 'starting points' of the developmental sequences are not attributed to individual genes, but rather to operations of the cell, or even to intercellular processes. (TZD, quoted in Sloan 2012: 148, my emphasis)

---

[76] This is a particularly consequential revelation, as TZD appeared in a German-language journal that was discontinued after only three issues—Delbrück later described the decision to publish it there as giving the paper "a funeral first class" (quoted in Sloan and Fogel 2011: 1). As a result, it is primarily through Schrödinger's exposition of it in *What Is Life?* that TZD has come to be known and interpreted (recall the claims made to this effect by both Waddington and Perutz, which we quoted in Section 3).

The failure to recognize this serious discordance between TZD and *What Is Life?* has meant that Delbrück's research program in biology (which stemmed from the desire to *confirm* Bohr's biological views) has often been erroneously equated with Schrödinger's (which stemmed from the desire to *refute* those very same views). This has caused widespread confusion. For example, Schrödinger's oft-quoted remark in *What Is Life?* that he expected 'new laws of physics' to be discovered in biology has tended to get conflated with Delbrück's Bohr-inspired search for a paradox that would reveal the limits of 'classical' descriptions of biological phenomena and require some form of complementarity to fully explain them (see Delbrück 1949). The first to make this unfortunate conflation appears to have been Stent (1966: 4), and many others have made the same mistake since (e.g., Carlson 1971: 152; Jacob 1973: 259; Perutz 1987b: 242; Davies 2019: 6; Sigmund 2019: 43).[77]

Returning to Schrödinger's genocentrism, the key point is that it was, at least to some extent, a *choice*. Schrödinger did not inevitably *arrive* at it after surveying the biological literature of the time. What the historical evidence indicates instead is that he first adopted it and *then* used it to decide what biological papers to read and how to interpret them. Yoxen has reported that Paul Ewald, the physicist who drew Schrödinger's attention to TZD in 1942, told him that "Schrödinger appeared not to be interested in a thorough survey of the literature in biology, but rather wanted to know of a few articles that would corroborate his point of view" (Yoxen 1979: 35), and also that Schrödinger's angry retort to Ewald's additional reading suggestions was: "'What do you think, I can't read the entire literature!'" (quoted in Yoxen 1977: 147).

What this implies is that, as I argued at the start of this section, there is nothing improper or unfair about taking Schrödinger to task for his unapologetically genocentric view of the cell. And the same could be said for his brazen disregard of the effects of stochasticity at the molecular level. As we noted in Section 5, the impact of random perturbations on microscopic processes has been a well-documented phenomenon—not just in physics but also in biology—for a very long time.[78] Indeed, it is not difficult to find extended discussions of it in the early twentieth-century literature (e.g., Thompson 1917). Thus, it would have been far from obvious in 1944 that one could realistically describe 'the physical aspect of the

---

[77] I am hardly the first to recognize this. Stent's conflation of Schrödinger's and Delbrück's respective agendas in biology was already noted and criticized in Fleming 1968 and in Olby 1974. McKaughan 2005 offers a more recent discussion of this conflation.

[78] Let us not forget that 'Brownian motion' is named after the botanist Robert Brown, who first reported it in 1827!

living cell' (not to mention the far more complex process of development) *without* acknowledging the disruptive effects of statistical fluctuations. In fact, Delbrück criticized Schrödinger's argument for precisely this reason in his 1945 review of *What Is Life?*:

> The author [i.e., Schrödinger] does not return in his later discussion to the problem of how the cell gets around the statistical fluctuations. *The careful reader will be disappointed by this omission.* At the beginning of the book the statistical fluctuations are represented as an unsurmountable obstacle to the physical understanding of the cell, but later on this difficulty seems forgotten. Without a finer discussion of this aspect, particularly for enzymatic processes and for non-steady states, the argument of the book loses its strength. (Delbrück 1945: 371, my emphasis)

Many commentators have complained that much of the biology that Schrödinger discussed in his book was already out of date even before he wrote it. But according to what I have argued in this section, this is not terribly surprising, and not even all that problematic. *What Is Life?* was never intended to advance biology; to judge it according to that standard is to fundamentally misunderstand why it was written. Schrödinger was a physicist, not a biologist. The biological argument he developed in the book, despite the impact it later happened to exert, was for Schrödinger simply a tool—a means to an end. Once he had made his point (even if it was lost on most of his readers!) he turned his attention to other matters. As Symonds (who studied with Schrödinger) puts it, "[s]omewhere along the line the problems tackled in *What Is Life?* confronted him, were thought about, the lectures were given and the book written, and then the episode was forgotten as he moved on to think about something else" (Symonds 1986: 226).[79]

This explains why, despite the encouragement (both publicly and in private correspondence) of leading geneticists such as Haldane and Darlington, Schrödinger never wrote about genetics again; even after describing it in *What Is Life?* as "easily the most interesting [science] of our days" (Schrödinger 1944: 41).[80] It also explains why he did not take the opportunity to properly update his book for its second edition of 1948—or at any point thereafter—in light of later biological discoveries, which

---

[79] Symonds also recounts that when Weaver visited Dublin in 1950, he had "hoped to discover that Schrödinger [maintained] a serious and active interest in applying various concepts of theoretical physics to biological problems". However, he was disappointed to be told by Schrödinger that *What Is Life?* had been "a purely personal venture" (Symonds 1986: 226).

[80] Schrödinger did briefly discuss genetics-related questions with Haldane (see Crow 1992) and with the botanist Irene Manton (see Williams 2016) following the publication of *What Is Life?*. And Yoxen (1977) has documented that he was subsequently invited to present the main ideas of his book to biological audiences in Cork, Manchester, and Alpbach.

he could have easily interpreted as decisive vindications of his argument (as I suggested in Section 5). And it is probably also why he did not bother responding to Crick's letter following the momentous discovery of the double helix in 1953 (recall Figure 3).[81]

7 Conclusions: *What Is Life?* 80 Years On

What Is Life? has become "part of the folklore of biology" (Symonds 1986: 221). The book keeps "providing nourishment for historians, sociologists and philosophers of science who have commented on it, [...] or on the comments on the comments on it" (Perutz 1987a: 555). Its popularity among scientists also shows no signs of abating. Morange (2020: 74) has recently remarked that "[m]odern molecular biologists feel quite at home studying the pages of Schrödinger's book" because "[t]hey share Schrödinger's determinist vision of the gene". 80 years on, the book continues to be widely read. It also remains widely misunderstood. We have seen that virtually all of the book's memorable expressions—'aperiodic crystal', 'hereditary code-script', 'negative entropy', 'new laws of physics'—have lent themselves to a fascinating array of interpretations, some more misleading than others. It appears that "[r]eaders of *What Is Life?*", as Olby (1974: 246) pithily observed, have "found in it what they were looking for". This should remind us to take autobiographical declarations of the book's influence (such as those collected in Box 1) with a grain of salt, though we should be equally wary of overly dismissive reassessments (like those of Perutz and Pauling, and of the historians that have followed in their footsteps) for the same reason.

Schrödinger's book offered a physical framework to think about two central features of life, heredity and metabolism, though he was evidently far more interested in the former than in the latter. Schrödinger's bias was embraced by the molecular biology pioneers who sought in *What Is Life?* a legitimation of their own concern with the molecular structure of the genetic material. It is interesting that many of these pioneers—most notably Delbrück and his group—used bacteriophage viruses as their experimental system, as these are purely parasitic, crystallizable entities in which the metabolic function has been lost and only the hereditary function survives. Dyson (1985: 5) has perceptively noted that in his book, "Schrödinger's view of what constitutes a living organism resembles a bacteriophage more

---

[81] Darlington actually recalls meeting Schrödinger around this time and, according to Olby (1970: 943), "found him apathetic about the problems he had earlier discussed with such enthusiasm".

than it resembles a bacterium or a fruit-fly", which in hindsight proved perfectly appropriate.[82]

The title of Schrödinger's book is too good, and too obvious, to have been original. Schrödinger was not the first to write a book titled *What Is Life?* (e.g., Windle 1908; Gaskell 1928), nor, for that matter, has he been the last (e.g., Margulis and Sagan 1995; Regis 2009; Pross 2012; Nurse 2021).[83] Even so, 'What is life?' has come to be almost universally regarded as 'Schrödinger's problem' (Olby 1971) or as 'Schrödinger's question' (Rosen 1996). This is amusing and ironic; not only because Schrödinger does not even try to answer 'his' question, but because one of the salient consequences of his book's success—and of the molecular revolution that ensued—was the banishment of that previously central question from the biological discourse (Shostak 1998; Morange 2008). As Jacob (1973: 299) famously declared, "[b]iologists no longer study life today". With the rise of molecular biology, the old concern with the organization of living systems was replaced with a new fixation on the structure and function of *genes*, which came to be viewed as the *master controllers of life*—just as Muller had envisioned in his 1929 manifesto.[84]

Without wanting to downplay the book's role in rallying young and disaffected physicists to the cause of elucidating the nature of the hereditary substance, I have suggested in this Element that we should not lose sight of the actual argument it put forward. *What Is Life?* should be remembered not simply because of *who* wrote it (despite the author's preeminent scientific reputation) but also because of *what* it claimed. As we have seen, the mechanical, deterministic, and genocentric view of the cell articulated in its pages was instrumental in shaping and consolidating the agenda of molecular biology during the second half of the twentieth century. Molecular biologists' conception of cellular order as organization-from-information is recognizably Schrödingerian, and so is their understanding of development as the execution of a pre-existing genetic program. Principles such as informational and structural specificity, the Central Dogma, and even the pervasive metaphorical appeals to molecular machines and solid-state electronic circuits can all be construed as theoretical extensions of

---

[82] This is even more remarkable when we consider that when Schrödinger wrote *What Is Life?* he was unaware that Delbrück had long abandoned the fruit fly in favor of the bacteriophage as his experimental system in genetics.

[83] Even the title of this Element is too good, and too obvious, to be new. 35 years ago, Sarkar penned a three-and-a-half page essay with the same title (i.e., Sarkar 1991).

[84] What Schrödinger is really asking in his book is not 'What is life?' but rather 'What is *controlling* life?'. This, incidentally, is the fitting title given to an edited volume that examined the legacy of *What Is Life?* 50 years on (Gnaiger et al. 1994).

the argument that Schrödinger laid out in *What Is Life?*—even if some emerged independently of it.

A key point to remember about Schrödinger's argument is that *it can be held empirically to account*. It might well have turned out to be true that cellular and organismic order is conserved and transmitted by means of a self-executing, preformationist code-script embedded in the solid-state structure of an aperiodic crystal that is immune to the ravages of thermal agitation. As it happens, however, there is now overwhelming empirical evidence that this is not in fact the case. In this respect, to think carefully about the problems with Schrödinger's argument—as we have done so in this Element—is to reflect on the limitations of conventional molecular biological explanations of macromolecular, cellular, and developmental phenomena.

Despite the book's popularity and influence, Schrödinger's original reasons for writing it have been completely forgotten—or so I have argued. The fact that his dispute with Jordan and Bohr regarding the extension of quantum mechanics to biology and psychology did not go anywhere shows, in a sense, how triumphant Schrödinger has been. Leaving aside the perennial problem of free will, which continues to be discussed today with as much vigour and panache as it was in the 1930s and 1940s (and, like most fundamental philosophical problems, is unlikely to ever be conclusively resolved), the empirical question of the bearing of quantum indeterminacy on cellular processes *was* decisively settled, and in Schrödinger's favour. Jordan's quantum biology faded into oblivion in the immediate post-war period, and molecular biologists have shown no appetite to reconsider the relevance of quantum effects ever since.[85]

I hope to have convincingly shown in this Element that philosophers, historians, and biologists all stand to benefit immeasurably from revisiting *What Is Life?* today. And not because what the book says is true, but because reading it helps us understand how we ended up with our current image of the cell, and how this image is likely to evolve in the decades to come. Recalling Judson's (1979: 244) remark, perhaps it is time, once again, that "[e]verybody read Schrödinger".

---

[85] There are some signs that quantum biology may be on the verge of a rebirth (see Ball 2011; McFadden and Al-Khalili 2014), but an examination of this intriguing prospect will need to be left for another occasion.

References

Abir-Am, P. 1985. Themes, genres, and orders of legitimation in the consolidation of new scientific disciplines: Deconstructing the historiography of molecular biology. *History of Science* 23: 73–117.

Akam, M. 1989. Making stripes inelegantly. *Nature* 341: 282–283.

Alberts, B. 1998. The cell as a collection of protein machines: Preparing the next generation of molecular biologists. *Cell* 92: 291–294.

Alexander, J. and Bridges, C. B. 1929. Some physicochemical aspects of life, mutation and evolution. *Science* 70: 508–510.

Anon. 1938. Prof. E. Schrödinger and the University of Graz. *Nature* 141: 929.

Ball, P. 2011. The dawn of quantum biology. *Nature* 474: 272–274.

  2015. Forging patterns and making waves from biology to geology: A commentary on Turing (1952) 'The chemical basis of morphogenesis'. *Philosophical Transactions of the Royal Society B* 370: 20140218. http://dx.doi.org/10.1098/rstb.2014.0218

  2018. In retrospect: *What Is Life? Nature* 560: 548–550.

  2023. *How Life Works: A User's Guide to the New Biology*. University of Chicago Press.

Będbenek, A, and Ziuzia-Graczyk, I. 2018. Fidelity of DNA replication – A matter of processing. *Current Genetics* 64: 985–996.

Benzer, S. 2002. Interview by Heidi Aspaturian. Oral History Project, California Institute of Technology Archives. https://digital.archives.caltech.edu/collections/OralHistories/OH_Benzer_S/

Bernstein, J. 2016. *A Bouquet of Numbers and Other Scientific Offerings*. World Scientific.

Beyler, R. H. 1994. From positivism to organicism: Pascual Jordan's interpretations of modern physics in cultural context. Dissertation, Harvard University.

  1996. Targeting the organism: The scientific and cultural context of Pascual Jordan's quantum biology, 1932–1947. *Isis* 87: 248–273.

Bialek, W., Cavagna, A., Giardina, I., Mora, T., Edmondo, S., Viale, M., and Walczak, A. M. 2012. Statistical mechanics for natural flocks of birds. *Proceedings of the National Academy of Sciences* 109: 4786–4791.

Bohr, N. 1999. *Collected Works, Vol. 10: Complementarity Beyond Physics (1928–1962)*. Elsevier.

Boltzmann, L. 1974. *Theoretical Physics and Philosophical Problems: Selected Writings*. Reidel.

Bondurianksy, R. and Day, T. 2018. *Extended Heredity: A New Understanding of Inheritance and Evolution*. Princeton University Press.

Boycott, A. E. 1929. The transition from live to dead: The nature of filtrable viruses. *Nature* 123: 91–98.

Brabazon. 1945. Causality or indeterminism? *Nature* 155: 398.

Brioullin, L. 1949. Life, thermodynamics, and cybernetics. *American Scientist* 37: 554–568.

——— 1956. *Science and Information Theory*. Academic Press.

Butler, J. A. V. 1946. Life and the second law of thermodynamics. *Nature* 158: 153–154.

Carlson, E. A. 1971. An unacknowledged founding of molecular biology: H. J. Muller's contributions to gene theory, 1910–1936. *Journal of the History of Biology* 4: 149–170.

Ceccarelli, L. 2001. *Shaping Science with Rhetoric: The Cases of Dobzhansky, Schrödinger, and Wilson*. University of Chicago Press.

Cairns, J., Stent, G. S., and Watson, J. D. 1966. *Phage and the Origins of Molecular Biology*. Cold Spring Harbor Laboratory Press.

Chargaff, E. 1978. *Heraclitean Fire: Sketches from a Life Before Nature*. Rockefeller University Press.

Clary, D. C. 2022. *Schrödinger in Oxford*. World Scientific.

Cobb, M. 2015. *Life's Greatest Secret: The Race to Crack the Genetic Code*. Profile.

Crick, F. H. C. 1958. On protein synthesis. *Symposium of the Society for Experimental Biology* 12: 138–163.

——— 1965. Recent research in molecular biology: Introduction. *British Medical Bulletin* 21: 183–186.

——— 1966. *Of Molecules and Men*. University of Washington Press.

Crow, J. F. 1992. Erwin Schrödinger and the hornless cattle problem. *Genetics* 130: 237–239.

Darlington, C. D. and Mather, K. 1950. *Genes, Plants and People: Essays on Genetics*. Allen & Unwin.

Davidson, E. H. 2009. Q&A. *Current Biology* 22: R216–R217.

Davies, P. 2019. *The Demon in the Machine: How Hidden Webs of Information Are Solving the Mystery of Life*. University of Chicago Press.

Dawkins, R. 1976. *The Selfish Gene*. Oxford University Press.

de Chadarevian, S. 1998. Of worms and programmes: *Caenorhabditis elegans* and the study of development. *Studies in History and Philosophy of Biological and Biomedical Sciences* 29: 81–105.

Deacon, T. W. 2011. *Incomplete Nature: How Mind Emerged from Matter*. W. W. Norton.

Delbrück, M. 1945. *What Is Life?* and what is truth? *Quarterly Review of Biology* 20: 370–372.

———. 1949. A physicist looks at biology. *Transactions of the Connecticut Academy of Arts and Sciences* 38: 173–190.

Depew, D. J. and Weber, B. H. 1995. *Darwinism Evolving: Systems Dynamics and the Geneaology of Natural Selection*. MIT Press.

Descartes, R. 1998. *The World and Other Writings*. Cambridge University Press.

Donnan, F. G. 1918. La science physico-chimique décrit-elle d'une façon adéquate les phénomènes biologiques? *Scientia* 24: 282–288.

———. 1928. The mystery of life. *Journal of Chemical Education* 122: 1558–1570.

———. 1936. Integral analysis and the phenomena of life. *Acta Biotheoretica* 2: 1–11.

Dowdle, E. B. 1989. Physics, Schrödinger and the study of life. *Transactions of the Royal Society of South Africa* 47: 103–108.

Dronamraju, K. R. 1999. Erwin Schrödinger and the origins of molecular biology. *Genetics* 153: 1071–1076.

Dyson, F. 1985. *Origins of Life*. Cambridge University Press.

Eldar, A. and Elowitz, M. B. 2010. Functional roles for noise in genetic circuits. *Nature* 467: 167–173.

Elitzur, A. C. 1995. Life and mind, past and future: Schrödinger's vision fifty years later. *Perspectives in Biology and Medicine* 38: 433–458.

Fischer, E. P. 1984. We are all aspects of one single being: An introduction to Erwin Schrödinger. *Social Research* 51: 809–835.

Fisher, R. A. 1930. *The Genetical Theory of Natural Selection*. Oxford University Press.

Fleming, D. 1968. Émigré physicists and the biological revolution. *Perspectives in American History* 2: 152–189.

Frank, J. 2011. *Molecular Machines in Biology: Workshop of the Cell*. Cambridge University Press.

Fuller, S. 2021. Schrödinger's *What Is Life?* as postdigital prophecy. *Postdigital Science and Education* 3: 272–279.

Gamow, G. 1953. *Mr. Tompkins Learns the Facts of Life*. Cambridge University Press.

———. 1955. Information transfer in the living cell. *Scientific American* 193: 70–78.

García-Ojalvo, J. and Martínez Arias, A. 2012. Towards a statistical mechanics of cell fate decisions. *Current Opinion in Genetics & Development* 22: 619–626.

Gaskell, A. 1928. *What Is Life?* Thomas Books.

Gehring, W. J. 1988. *Master Control Genes in Development and Evolution: The Homeobox Story.* Yale University Press.

Gierer, A. and Meinhardt, H. 1972. A theory of biological pattern formation. *Kybernetik* 12: 30–39.

Gilbert, W. 1992. A vision of the grail. In D. J. Kevles and L. Hood (eds.), *The Code of Codes: Scientific and Social Issues in the Human Genome Project.* Harvard University Press, pp. 83–97.

Gnaiger, E., Gellerich, F. N., and Wyss, M. 1994. *What Is Controlling Life? 50 Years After Erwin Schrödinger's What Is Life?* Innsbruck University Press.

Gould, S. J. 1995. What Is Life? as a problem in history. In M. P. Murphy and L. A. J. O'Neill (eds.), *What Is Life? The Next Fifty Years.* Cambridge University Press, pp. 25–39.

Gribbin, J. 2013. *Erwin Schrödinger and the Quantum Revolution.* Wiley.

Green, J. B. A. and Sharpe, J. 2015. Positional information and reaction-diffusion: Two big ideas in developmental biology combine. *Development* 142: 1203–1211.

Hacking, I. 1990. *The Taming of Chance.* Cambridge University Press.

Haldane, J. B. S. 1945. A physicist looks at genetics. *Nature* 155: 375–376.

Halpern, P. 2015. *Einstein's Dice and Schrödinger's Cat: How Two Great Minds Battled Quantum Randomness to Create a Unified Theory of Physics.* Basic Books.

Harrison, L. G. 1987. What is the status of reaction-diffusion theory thirty-four years after Turing? *Journal of Theoretical Biology* 125: 369–384.

Heams, T. 2014. Randomness in biology. *Mathematical Structures in Computer Science* 24: 1–24.

Heitler, W. 1961. Erwin Schrödinger (1887–1961). *Biographical Memoirs of Fellows of the Royal Society* 7: 221–228.

Hendrickson, M. R. 2011. Exorcizing Schrödinger's ghost: Reflections on *What Is Life?* and its surprising relevance to cancer biology. In H. U. Gumbrecht, R. P. Harrison, M. R. Hendrickson, and R. B. Laughlin (eds.), *What Is Life? The Intellectual Pertinence of Erwin Schrödinger.* Stanford University Press, pp. 45–103.

Hetler, D. M. and Bronfenbrenner, J. 1929. On the particulate size of bacteriophage. *Proceedings of the Society for Experimental Biology and Medicine* 26: 644–645.

Hoch, P. K. and Yoxen, E. J. 1987. Schrödinger at Oxford: A hypothetical national cultural synthesis which failed. *Annals of Science* 44: 593–616.

Hodge, M. J. S. 1992. Biology and philosophy (including ideology): A study of Fisher and Wright. In S. Sarkar (ed.), *The Founders of Evolutionary Genetics*. Kluwer, pp. 231–293.

Huang, S. 2009. Non-genetic heterogeneity of cells in development: More than just noise. *Development* 136: 3853–3862.

Jablonka, E. and Lamb, M. J. 2014. *Evolution in Four Dimensions: Genetic, Epigenetic, Behavioral, and Symbolic Variation in the History of Life* (rev. ed.). MIT Press.

Jacob, F. 1973. *The Logic of Life: A History of Heredity*. Pantheon.

1988. *The Statue Within: An Autobiography*. Basic Books.

Jacob, F. and Monod, J. 1961. Genetic regulatory mechanisms in the synthesis of proteins. *Journal of Molecular Biology* 3: 318–356.

Johannsen, W. 1923. Some remarks about units in heredity. *Hereditas* 4: 133–141.

Jordan, P. 1932. Die Quantenmechanik und die Grundprobleme der Biologie und Psychologie. *Die Naturwissenschaften* 20: 815–821.

Judson, H. F. 1979. *The Eighth Day of Creation: Makers of the Revolution in Biology*. Simon & Schuster.

Kalmus, H. 1950. A cybernetical aspect of genetics. *Journal of Heredity* 41: 19–22.

Karsenti, E. 2008. Self-organization in cell biology: A brief history. *Nature Reviews Molecular Cell Biology* 9: 255–262.

Kauffman, S. 1995. *What Is Life?*: Was Schrödinger right? In M. P. Murphy and L. A. J. O'Neill (eds.), *What Is Life? The Next Fifty Years*. Cambridge University Press, pp. 83–114.

2000. *Investigations*. Oxford University Press.

Kay, L. E. 1985. The secret of life: Niels Bohr's influence on the biology program of Max Delbrück. *Rivista di Storia della Scienza* 2: 487–510.

1993. *The Molecular Vision of Life: Caltech, the Rockefeller Foundation, and the Rise of the New Biology*. Oxford University Press.

2000. *Who Wrote the Book of Life? A History of the Genetic Code*. Stanford University Press.

Keller, E. F. 1990. Physics and the emergence of molecular biology: A history of cognitive and political synergy. *Journal of the History of Biology* 23: 389–409.

1995. *Refiguring Life: Metaphors of Twentieth-Century Biology*. Columbia University Press.

2000. *The Century of the Gene*. Harvard University Press.

2002. *Making Sense of Life: Explaining Biological Development with Models, Metaphors, and Machines*. Harvard University Press.

2008. Organisms, machines, and thunderstorms: A history of self-organization, part one. *Historical Studies in the Natural Sciences* 38: 45–75.

2009. Organisms, machines, and thunderstorms: A history of self-organization, part two. *Historical Studies in the Natural Sciences* 39: 1–31.

Kendrew, J. C. 1967. How molecular biology started. *Scientific American* 216: 141–144.

Kilmister, C. W. 1987. *Schrödinger: Centenary Celebration of a Polymath*. Cambridge University Press.

Kirschner, M., Gerhart, M., and Mitchison, T. 2000. Molecular 'vitalism'. *Cell* 100: 79–88.

Kogge, W. 2012. Script, code, information: How to differentiate analogies in the 'prehistory' of molecular biology. *History and Philosophy of the Life Sciences* 34: 604–635.

Kondo, S. and Miura, T. 2010. Reaction-diffusion model as a framework for understanding biological pattern formation. *Science* 329: 1616–1620.

Kupiec, J.-J. 2009. *The Origin of Individuals*. World Scientific.

2010. On the lack of specificity of proteins and its consequences for a theory of biological organization. *Progress in Biophysics and Molecular Biology* 102: 45–52.

Laughlin, R. B. 2011. Schrödinger's trouble: How quantum mechanics got created with a logical loose end. In H. U. Gumbrecht, R. P. Harrison, M. R. Hendrickson, and R. B. Laughlin (eds.), *What Is Life? The Intellectual Pertinence of Erwin Schrödinger*. Stanford University Press, pp. 33–43.

Lewontin, R. C. 1968. Essay review: Phage and the origins of molecular biology. *Journal of the History of Biology* 1: 155–161.

1970. The units of selection. *Annual Review of Ecology and Systematics* 1: 1–18.

2000. *The Triple Helix: Gene, Organism, and Environment*. Harvard University Press.

Loison, L. 2015. Why did Jacques Monod make the choice of mechanistic determinism? *Comptes Rendus Biologies* 338: 391–397.

Longo, G. and Tendero, P. E. 2007. The differential method and the causal incompleteness of programming theory in molecular biology. *Foundations of Science* 12: 337–366.

Lovelock, J. A. 1986. Living alternatives. *Nature* 320: 646.

1988. *The Ages of Gaia: A Biography of Our Living Earth*. Oxford University Press.

Lwoff, A. 1962. *Biological Order*. MIT Press.
MacArthur, B. D. and Lemischka, I. R. 2013. Statistical mechanics of pluripotency. *Cell* 154: 484–489.
MacKenzie, D. A. 1981. *Statistics in Britain (1865–1930): The Social Construction of Scientific Knowledge*. Edinburgh University Press.
Maini, P. K. 2004. The impact of Turing's work on pattern formation in biology. *Mathematics Today* 40: 140–141.
Manton, I. 1945. Comments on chromosome structure. *Nature* 155: 471–473.
Margulis, L. and Sagan, D. 1995. *What Is Life?* University of California Press.
Maynard Smith, J. 1968. *Mathematical Ideas in Biology*. Cambridge University Press.
Mayr, E. 1961. Cause and effect in biology. *Science* 134: 1501–1506.
— 1997. *This Is Biology: The Science of the Living World*. Harvard University Press.
McFadden, J. and Al-Khalili, J. 2014. *Life on the Edge: The Coming of Age of Quantum Biology*. Crown Publishers.
McKaughan, D. J. 2005. The influence of Niels Bohr on Max Delbrück: Revisiting the hopes inspired by "Light and Life". *Isis* 96: 507–529.
Medawar, P. 1965. A biological retrospect. *Nature* 207: 1327–1330.
Mertens, R. 2019. *The Construction of Analogy-Based Research Programs: The Lock-and-Key Analogy in 20th Century Biochemistry*. Transcript Verlag.
Moberg, C. 2020. Schrödinger's *What Is Life?* – The 75th anniversary of a book that inspired biology. *Angewandte Chemie* 59: 2550–2553.
Monod, J. 1966. L'être vivant comme machine. In R. Caillois (ed.), *Le Robot, la Bête et l'Homme*. Baconnière, pp. 43–47.
— 1972. *Chance and Necessity: An Essay on the Natural Philosophy of Molecular Biology*. New Vintage.
— 2021 [1960]. *Cybérnetique Enzymatique*. Èditions Matériologiques.
Moore, W. 1989. *Schrödinger: Life and Thought*. Cambridge University Press.
Moore, P. B. 2012. How should we think about the ribosome? *Annual Review of Biophysics* 41: 1–19.
Morange, M. 2008. *Life Explained*. Odile Jacob.
— 2020. *The Black Box of Biology: A History of the Molecular Revolution*. Harvard University Press.
Morowitz, H. J. 1970. *Entropy for Biologists*. Academic Press.
Moss, L. 2003. *What Genes Can't Do*. MIT Press.
Muller, H. J. 1922. Variation due to change in the individual gene. *American Naturalist* 56: 32–50.

1929. The gene as the basis of life. *Proceedings of the International Congress of Plant Sciences* 1: 897–921.

1937. Physics in the attack on the fundamental problems of genetics. *Scientific Monthly* 44: 210–214.

1946. A physicist stands amazed at genetics. *Journal of Heredity* 32: 90–92.

Murphy, M. P. and O'Neill L. A. J. 1995. *What Is Life? The Next Fifty Years*. Cambridge University Press.

Needham, J. 1936. *Order and Life*. Cambridge University Press.

Newman, S. A. 1988. Idealist biology. *Perspectives in Biology and Medicine* 31: 353–368.

Nicholson, D. J. 2014. The machine conception of the organism in development and evolution: A critical analysis. *Studies in History and Philosophy of Biological and Biomedical Sciences* 48: 162–174.

2018. Reconceptualizing the organism: From complex machine to flowing stream. In D. J. Nicholson and J. Dupré (eds.), *Everything Flows: Towards a Processual Philosophy of Biology*. Oxford University Press, pp. 139–166.

2019. Is the cell *really* a machine? *Journal of Theoretical Biology* 477: 108–126.

2020. On being the right size, revisited: The problem with engineering metaphors in molecular biology. In S. Holm and M. Serban (eds.), *Philosophical Perspectives on the Engineering Approach in Biology: Living Machines?* Routledge, pp. 40–68.

Nicolis, G. and Prigogine, I. 1977. *Self-Organization in Non-Equilibrium Systems*. Wiley.

Nijhout, H. F. 1990. Metaphors and the role of genes in development. *BioEssays* 12: 441–446.

Noble, D. 2016. *Dance to the Tune of Life – Biological Relativity*. Cambridge University Press.

Nurse, P. 2021. *What Is Life? Five Great Ideas in Biology*. W. W. Norton.

O'Dwyer, J. P. 2020. Beyond an ecological ideal gas law. *Nature Ecology & Evolution* 4: 14–15.

Olby, R. 1970. Francis Crick, DNA, and the Central Dogma. *Daedalus* 99: 938–987.

1971. Schrödinger's problem: What is life? *Journal of the History of Biology* 4: 119–148.

1974. *The Path to the Double Helix*. University of Washington Press.

Oparin, A. I. 1961. *Life: Its Nature, Origin and Development*. Oliver & Boyd.

Oyama, S., Griffiths, P. E., and Gray, R. D. 2001. *Cycles of Contingency: Developmental Systems and Evolution*. MIT Press.

Pauling, L. 1987. Schrödinger's contribution to chemistry and biology. In C. W. Kilmister (ed.), *Schrödinger: Centenary Celebration of a Polymath*. Cambridge University Press, pp. 225–233.

Pence, C. H. 2022. *The Rise of Chance in Evolutionary Theory: A Pompous Parade of Arithmetic*. Academic Press.

Perutz, M. F. 1987a. Physics and the riddle of life. *Nature* 326: 555–558.

1987b. Erwin Schrödinger's *What Is Life?* and molecular biology. In C. W. Kilmister (ed.), *Schrödinger: Centenary Celebration of a Polymath*. Cambridge University Press, pp. 234–251.

Phillips, R. 2021. Schrödinger's *What Is Life?* at 75. *Cell Systems* 12: 465–476.

Pollard, E. C. 1967. Erwin Schrödinger (1887–1961). In F. M. Snell (ed.), *Progress in Theoretical Biology, Vol. 1*. Academic Press, pp. ix–xi.

Porter, T. M. 1986. *The Rise of Statistical Thinking (1820–1900)*. Princeton University Press.

Prigogine, I. and Stengers, I. 1984. *Order Out of Chaos: Man's New Dialogue with Nature*. Bantam.

Pross, A. 2012. *What Is Life? How Chemistry Becomes Biology*. Oxford University Press.

Quastler, H. 1953. *Essays on the Use of Information Theory in Biology*. University of Illinois Press.

Regis, E. 2009. *What Is Life? Investigating the Nature of Life in the Age of Synthetic Biology*. Oxford University Press.

Reitz, J. R. and Longmire, C. 1950. Living matter and physical laws. *Physics Today* 3: 15–19.

Roll-Hansen, N. 2000. The application of complementarity to biology: From Niels Bohr to Max Delbrück. *Historical Studies in the Physical and Biological Sciences* 30: 417–442.

Rose, S. 1998. *Lifelines: Biology Beyond Determinism*. Oxford University Press.

Rosen, R. 1996. The Schrödinger question: What is life? Fifty years later. In P. Buckley and F. D. Peat (eds.). *Glimpsing Reality: Ideas in Physics and the Link to Biology*. University of Toronto Press, pp. 168–190.

Rosenberg, A. 1997. Reductionism redux: Computing the embryo. *Biology and Philosophy* 12: 445–470.

Sarkar, S. 1991. *What Is Life?* revisited. *BioScience* 41: 631–634.

1996. Biological information: A skeptical look at some central dogmas of molecular biology. In S. Sarkar (ed.), *The Philosophy and History of Molecular Biology*. Springer, pp. 187–231.

2013. Erwin Schrödinger's excursus on genetics. In O. Harman and M. R. Dietrich (eds.), *Outsider Scientists: Routes to Innovation in Biology*. University of Chicago Press, pp. 93–109.

Schneider, E. D. 1987. Schrödinger's grand theme shortchanged. *Nature* 328: 300.

Schneider, E. D. and Kay, J. J. 1994. Life as a manifestation of the second law of thermodynamics. *Mathematical and Computer Modeling* 19: 25–48.

Schneider, E. D. and Sagan, D. 2005. *Into the Cool: Energy Flow, Thermodynamics, and Life*. University of Chicago Press.

Schoenheimer, R. 1942. *The Dynamic State of Body Constituents*. Harvard University Press.

Schrödinger, E. 1933. Warum sind die Atome so klein? *Forschungen und Fortschritte* 9: 125–126.

1935a. Die gegenwärtige Situation in der Quantenmechanik. *Naturwissenschaften* 23: 807–812, 823–828, 844–849.

1935b. *Science and the Human Temperament*. Allen & Unwin.

1936. Indeterminism and free will. *Nature* 138: 13–14.

1944. *What Is Life? The Physical Aspect of the Living Cell*. Cambridge University Press.

1946. *Statistical Thermodynamics*. Cambridge University Press.

1951. *Science and Humanism: Physics in Our Time*. Cambridge University Press.

1954. *Nature and the Greeks*. Cambridge University Press.

1958. *Mind and Matter*. Cambridge University Press.

1964. *My View of the World*. Cambridge University Press.

1992. *What Is Life? with Mind and Matter and Autobiographical Sketches*. Cambridge University Press.

Semon, R. 1904. *Die Mneme als erhaltendes Prinzip*. Engemann.

Shannon, C. 1956. The bandwagon. *IRE Transactions on Information Theory IT* 2: 3.

Shannon, C. and Weaver, W. 1949. *The Mathematical Theory of Communication*. University of Illinois Press.

Shostak, S. 1998. *Death of Life: The Legacy of Molecular Biology*. Macmillan.

Sigmund, K. 2019. The physicist and the dawn of the double helix. *Science* 366: 43.

Sloan, P. R. 2012. How was teleology eliminated in early molecular biology? *Studies in History and Philosophy of Biological and Biomedical Sciences* 43: 140–151.

2025. A return to Niels Bohr's 'Light and Life' (1932). *Biological Theory.* https://doi.org/10.1007/s13752-025-00490-y

Sloan, P. R. and Fogel, B. 2011. *Creating a Physical Biology: The Three-Man Paper and Early Molecular Biology.* University of Chicago Press.

Stent, G. S. 1966. Introduction: Waiting for the paradox. In J. Cairns, G. S. Stent, and J. D. Watson (eds.), *Phage and the Origins of Molecular Biology.* Cold Spring Harbor Laboratory Press, pp. 3–8.

1968. That was the molecular biology that was. *Science* 160: 390–395.

Sulston, J. E., Schierenberg, E., White, J. G., and Thomson, J. N. 1983. The embryonic cell lineage of the nematode *Caenorhabditis elegans. Developmental Biology* 100: 64–119.

Summers, W. C. 2023. *The American Phage Group: Founders of Molecular Biology.* Yale University Press.

Symonds, N. 1986. *What Is Life?* Schrödinger's influence on biology. *Quarterly Review of Biology* 61: 221–226.

Teschendorff, A. E. and Feinberg, A. P. 2021. Statistical mechanics meets single-cell biology. *Nature Reviews Genetics* 22: 459–476.

Thompson, D. W. 1917. *On Growth and Form.* Cambridge University Press.

Timoféeff-Ressovsky, N., Zimmer, K., and Delbrück, M. 1935. Über die Natur der Genmutation und der Genstruktur. *Nachrichten aus der Biologie der Gesellschaft der Wissenschaften zu Göttingen* 1: 189–245.

Tribus, M. and McIrvine, E. C. 1971. Energy and information. *Scientific American* 225: 179–188.

Turing, A. 1952. The chemical basis of morphogenesis. *Philosophical Transactions of the Royal Society B: Biological Sciences* 237: 37–72.

von Foerster, H. 1960. On self-organizing systems and their environments. In M. C. Yovits and S. Cameron (eds.), *Self-Organizing Systems.* Pergamon Press, pp. 31–50.

von Wright, G. H. 1955. Ludwig Wittgenstein, a biographical sketch. *Philosophical Review* 64: 527–545.

Waddington, C. H. 1962. *New Patterns in Genetics and Development.* Columbia University Press.

1969. Some European contributions to the prehistory of molecular biology. *Nature* 221: 318–321.

Walsby, A. E. and Hodge, M. J. S. 2017. Schrödinger's code-script: Not a genetic cipher but a code of development. *Studies in History and Philosophy of Biological and Biomedical Sciences* 63: 45–54.

Walsh, D. M. 2015. *Organism, Agency, and Evolution.* Cambridge University Press.

2020. Action, program, metaphor. *Interdisciplinary Science Reviews* 45: 344–359.

Watson, J. D. 1965. *The Molecular Biology of the Gene*. W. A. Benjamin, Inc.

1966. Growing up in the phage group. In J. Cairns, G. S. Stent, and J. D. Watson (eds.), *Phage and the Origins of Molecular Biology*. Cold Spring Harbor Laboratory Press, pp. 239–245.

1993. Succeeding in science: Some rules of thumb. *Science* 261: 1812–1813.

2001. *A Passion for DNA*. Cold Spring Harbor Laboratory Press.

Watson, J. D. and Crick, F. H. C. 1953a. Molecular structure of nucleic acids. *Nature* 171: 737–738.

1953b. Genetical implications of the structure of deoxyribonucleic acid. *Nature* 171: 964–967.

Weaver, W. 1948. Science and complexity. *American Scientist* 36: 536–544.

Weismann, A. 1893. *The Germ-Plasm: A Theory of Heredity*. Charles Scribner's Sons.

Weiss, P. A. 1973. *The Science of Life: The Living System – A System for Living*. Futura.

Wicken, J. 1987. *Evolution, Thermodynamics, and Information: Extending the Darwinian Program*. Oxford University Press.

Wiener, N. 1948. *Cybernetics: Control and Communication in the Animal and the Machine*. MIT Press.

Wigner, E. P. and Hodgkin, R. A. 1977. Michael Polanyi (1891–1976). *Biographical Memoirs of Fellows of the Royal Society* 23: 413–448.

Williams, N. 2016. Irene Manton, Erwin Schrödinger and the puzzle of chromosome structure. *Journal of the History of Biology* 49: 425–459.

Wilkins, M. H. F. 1963. Molecular configuration of nucleic acids. *Science* 140: 941–950.

Windle, B. C. A. 1908. *What Is Life? A Study of Vitalism and Neo-Vitalism*. Sands.

Wise, M. N. 1994. Pascual Jordan: Quantum mechanics, psychology, National Socialism. In M. Renneberg and M. Walker (eds.), *Science, Technology, and National Socialism*. Cambridge University Press, pp. 224–254.

Witkowski, J. A. 1986. Schrödinger's *What Is Life?*: Entropy, order, and hereditary code-scripts. *Trends in Biochemical Sciences* 11: 266–268.

Woese, C. R. 2004. A new biology for a new century. *Microbiology and Molecular Biology Reviews* 68: 173–186.

Wolpert, L. 1994. Do we understand development? *Science* 266: 571–572.

Wolpert, L. and Lewis, J. H. 1975. Towards a theory of development. In G. J. Thorbeke (ed.), *Biology of Aging and Development*. Faseb, pp. 21–34.

Wu, D., Daugherty, S. C., Van Aken, S. E., Pai, G. H., Watkins, K. L., Khouri, H., Tallon, L. J., Zaborsky, J. M., Dunbar, H. E., Tran, P. L., Moran, M. A., and Eisen, K. A. 2006. Metabolic complementarity and genomics of the dual bacterial symbiosis of sharpshooters. *PLoS Biology* 4: e188.

Yoxen, E. J. 1977. The social impact of molecular biology. Dissertation, University of Cambridge.

    1979. Where does Schrödinger's *What Is Life?* belong in the history of molecular biology? *History of Science* 17: 17–52.

Acknowledgements

My first and greatest debt of gratitude is to my wife, Eva, for holding the rope firmly as I threw myself with abandon into the bottomless Schrödingerian pit—and for pulling me out when the demands of real life required it.

I have benefitted enormously from many stimulating discussions with numerous colleagues over the years. I especially want to thank Phil Sloan, Laurent Loison, Jean-Jacques Kupiec, Lenny Moss, Stuart Newman, Karl Sigmund, Gerd Müller, Michel Morange, Jonathan Hodge, Andràs Paldi, Predrag Šustar, Charles Pence, Patricia Palacios, Gregor Greslehner, James DiFrisco, Richard Gawne, Frank Zachos, Jon Umerez, David Teira, Mauricio Suárez, Antonio Lazcano, Francisco Vergara-Silva, and Alejandro Fábregas-Tejeda.

I have also received helpful feedback on presentations of this project from audiences around the world, specifically in Oslo, Rijeka, Madrid, Vienna, Mexico City, Leuven, Santiago de Chile, Paris, Bochum, Louvain-la-Neuve, Lyon, Annapolis, and Cold Spring Harbor Laboratory (CSHL). My talk at CSHL was attended by the legendary James Watson—then 94 years of age—who was appalled that I had the audacity to criticize molecular biology's Schrödingerian view of the cell. Paradoxically, I found Watson's complaints rather reassuring, as they showed that I am not attacking a strawman.

On the historical side of the project, I am grateful to the staff at the following libraries and archives for their assistance: the Austrian Central Library for Physics in Vienna, the Dublin Institute for Advanced Studies, the Special Collections at University College London, the Berlin State Library, the Pasteur Institute in Paris, Cambridge University Library, and the CSHL Center for Humanities and History of Modern Biology.

Part of this Element was written while I was a Visiting Fellow at the Center for Philosophy of Science at the University of Pittsburgh, which provided an ideal environment in which to write. Special thanks to Edouard Machery and to the rest of the Fellows at the Center for their wonderfully insightful comments on an early draft. Victor García Sanabria provided invaluable support preparing the figures. Finally, I thank Grant Ramsey and the late Michael Ruse for their enthusiasm for this project.

The research undertaken for this Element was financially supported by a Sydney Brenner Fellowship at CSHL, and by the Institute for Philosophy and Public Policy at George Mason University.

Cambridge Elements

Philosophy of Biology

Grant Ramsey
KU Leuven

Grant Ramsey is a BOFZAP research professor at the Institute of Philosophy, KU Leuven, Belgium. His work centers on philosophical problems at the foundation of evolutionary biology. He has been awarded the Popper Prize twice for his work in this area. He also publishes in the philosophy of animal behavior, human nature and the moral emotions. He runs the Ramsey Lab (theramseylab.org), a highly collaborative research group focused on issues in the philosophy of the life sciences.

About the Series
This Cambridge Elements series provides concise and structured introductions to all of the central topics in the philosophy of biology. Contributors to the series are cutting-edge researchers who offer balanced, comprehensive coverage of multiple perspectives, while also developing new ideas and arguments from a unique viewpoint.

Cambridge Elements

Philosophy of Biology

Elements in the Series

Animal Models of Human Disease
Sara Green

Cultural Selection
Tim Lewens

Biological Organization
Leonardo Bich

Controlled Experiments
Jutta Schickore

Slime Mould and Philosophy
Matthew Sims

Explanation in Biology
Lauren N. Ross

Philosophy of Physiology
Maël Lemoine

The Organism
Jan Baedke

Human Cognitive Diversity
Ingo Brigandt

Modelling Evolution
Walter Veit

The Scope of Evolutionary Thinking
Thomas A. C. Reydon

What Is Life? Revisited
Daniel J. Nicholson

A full series listing is available at: www.cambridge.org/EPBY

Made in the USA
Monee, IL
03 May 2026

49437534R00059